RAPID
REALIGNMENT

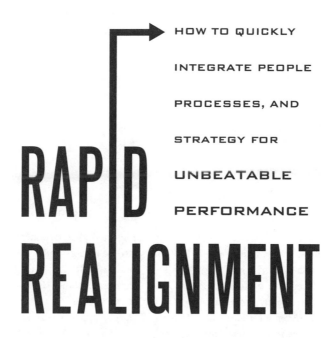

HOW TO QUICKLY

INTEGRATE PEOPLE

PROCESSES, AND

STRATEGY FOR

RAPID

UNBEATABLE

PERFORMANCE

REALIGNMENT

GEORGE LABOVITZ
VICTOR ROSANSKY

New York   Chicago   San Francisco   Lisbon   London
Madrid   Mexico City   Milan   New Delhi   San Juan
Seoul   Singapore   Sydney   Toronto

1 2 3 4 5 6 7 8 9 0   DOC/DOC   1 8 7 6 5 4 3 2

ISBN: 978-0-07-179113-7
MHID: 0-07-179113-2

e-ISBN: 978-0-07-179114-4
e-MHID: 0-07-179114-0

This publication is designed to provide accurate and authoritative information in
regard to the subject matter covered. It is sold with the understanding that neither
the author nor the publisher is engaged in rendering legal, accounting, or other
professional service. If legal advice or other expert assistance is required, the
services of a competent professional person should be sought.
　　　　—From a Declaration of Principles Jointly Adopted by a Committee of the
　　　American Bar Association and a Committee of Publishers and Associations

McGraw-Hill books are available at special quantity discounts to use as premiums and
sales promotions, or for use in corporate training programs. To contact a representative,
please e-mail us at bulksales@mcgraw-hill.com.

This book is printed on acid-free paper.

Contents

Acknowledgments

This book represents the evolution of our thinking over many years of working with some of the smartest leaders and thinkers we have had the privilege to know. It would be a daunting, if not hopeless, task to thank all the colleagues, clients, and friends who have influenced and contributed to the development of our ideas and concepts. There are a number of people, however, to whom we would like to give special acknowledgment and thanks for providing the inspiration for this book and the sweat it took to produce it.

First, the sweat.

Without the help of Richard Luecke's writing and editing skills, this book would be a pale imitation of the final product. A wonderful colleague and occasional taskmaster, he kept us focused and out of the rabbit holes we might have fallen into if left to our own devices. Lynn Johnston, our book agent, provided critical help in clarifying the organization and presentation of our material.

Professor Lloyd Baird, a colleague at the Boston University School of Management, reviewed the manuscript and made many constructive suggestions—so constructive that we incorporated most of them into the text. Another colleague, Professor John McCarthy, provided valuable insights and shared with us his example of a company struggling with a traumatic transition. Their boss, Dean Ken Freeman, was generous with his time, support, and insights and provided an excellent case example.

Stan Labovitz, George's brother, runs a company called InfoTool. He provided valuable ongoing suggestions and support and is a partner in our alignment measurement work.

Our ODI colleagues Alan Burleson and Jane Joyce added content, as well as support and organization, to our efforts. Lynne Rosansky, wearing her hat as organizational anthropologist, suffered through endless discussions on the role of culture in alignment and offered suggestions that greatly improved the subject matter.

Now, the inspiration.

Each of the leaders we included in the book provided a model of what we feel is necessary to align, realign, and mobilize an organization, including very large ones. In particular, we owe a debt to Fred Smith, the Chairman of FedEx, and to Admiral Vern Clark, the now retired Chief of Naval Operations. Although they were clients of ours, we were nevertheless students of theirs. Much of what we've learned from them about leading alignment is reflected in the pages of this book.

In our work with the U.S. Navy, we had the privilege of working with a number of senior leaders who provided rich examples and lessons for us and our readers, including now retired Vice Admirals Wally Massenburg, Tim LaFleur, and Phil Balisle, and Captain Mitch Heroman.

Admirals Mark "Lobster" Fitzgerald (retired) and Sam Locklear, and Vice Admiral (retired) Ed Zortman showed us the power of alignment in practice—especially when Sam Locklear, then commanding the Nimitz Battle Group, declared, "Align or die!"

Dr. James Mandell, CEO of Children's Hospital Boston, Dr. Ed Benz, Jr., CEO of Dana-Farber Cancer Institute, and Sandra Fenwick, President and COO of Children's Hospital, were most generous with their time and insights. They also provided us with an excellent example of enterprise leadership. Bill Margaritis, Senior Vice President of Global Communications at FedEx, was most helpful in providing material and guidance, especially in the area of measurement.

The impact of culture from a global perspective was illuminated by Mustafa Abdel-Wadood, CEO of Abraaj Capital. Irving

Wladawsky-Berger, former IBM Vice President of Technical Strategy and Innovation, provided valuable perspective on the challenges of culture in organizational transformations.

The late Sam Walton, founder of Walmart, and Tom Laco, the now-retired Vice Chairman at Procter & Gamble, provided seasoned business acumen early in our process of thinking about the importance of alignment in business relationships. Earl Conway, P&G's former Corporate Head of Quality, was a thought leader on the importance of alignment in total quality management. Peter Nolan, former Senior Vice President of Sales and Marketing for Electrolux Europe, helped develop the notion of partnering as a means for businesses to develop new working models.

And over the years, our many ODI colleagues kept moving our thinking forward. Special thanks goes to Dr. Yu Sang Chang, coauthor of our first book, Making Quality Work, who taught us the value of converting problems into "treasures," to Kevin Smith, ODI Australia, and to William Keyser, ODI UK, whoprovided fertile grounds for developing ideas. Stephanie Goode provided valuable insights on alignment and culture.

With sadness we would also like to acknowledge the passing of our friend and colleague, Dr. George Weathersby, who worked with us during our four-year tour of alignment consulting "duty" with the U.S. Navy. A world-class scholar and executive, he added numerous insights to our understanding of how alignment can be measured and how those measures correlate with operational performance. We will miss him.

Finally, George Labovitz, a former Air Force pilot, wants to acknowledge the men and women of our armed forces as a primary source of inspiration. "Working with them was a 'back in the day' experience for me. In many ways, the military personifies both the necessary imperative and the positive outcomes of alignment. I hope that our work, in some small way, has helped to make them more effective, more productive, and, above all, safer."

George Labovitz   *Victor Rosansky*

Introduction

When Admiral Vern Clark became Chief of Naval Operations in 2001, he inherited an enormous, diverse organization of over 900,000 people with a budget approaching $100 billion. It was also an organization jokingly known for "two hundred years of tradition, unhampered by progress." The U.S. Navy was in fact many navies. There was an undersea Navy, a surface Navy, an aviation Navy, a Pacific Navy, and an Atlantic Navy. Each had its own culture, and each operated with great independence.

As the top guy in the Navy, Clark could sense enormous misalignment in his organization and recognized what it was costing the service in terms of performance and money. At any given time almost 40 percent of the Navy's aircraft were nonoperational, and trained personnel were leaving in droves. The reenlistment rate for people who had completed their initial tours of service was around 19 percent, which meant that approximately 80 percent were walking away with the years of training and experience they'd acquired at taxpayer expense. More important, attrition (failing to complete their agreed-to service) of first-term sailors was approaching 40 percent. "Things were broken in ways that nobody knew," Clark explained. "The Navy was hollowing out. It was my sense," he told us, "that if we were a public company, we'd have been in Chapter 11."

Admiral Clark wanted to take apart his Navy of ships and planes, facilities and people, and put it back together in a way that would let it operate with seamless efficiency and effectiveness. For him, the U.S. Navy had a clear and unambiguous Main Thing: victory in combat. And there was no room for second place in that serious business. He was prepared to devote his tenure as CNO to aligning the Navy, enhancing its readiness, and improving its ability to work jointly with the other military services.

Upon assuming command, Clark set five major goals, and alignment was one of them. He made our earlier book, *The Power of Alignment*, required reading for all of his admirals. He felt that the alignment framework upon which that book was based gave him, in his words, "a framework on which to hang my leadership." When we pointed out that over 30 years of empirical research showed that aligned organizations outperform their nearest competitors by every major financial measure, he responded by saying, "That may be true, but the reason I made alignment one of the Navy's five goals was that, in *my* business, second place is a terminal disease."

Then came the war on terrorism.

Suddenly, the pace of change increased. Clark's response to the war on terror was to better align the Navy with its ultimate purpose: victory in combat. The Navy's role in the war on terror necessitated a dramatic change in strategy, tactics, and weapons. Clark had to set a new direction for the Navy, reconfigure its traditional war-fighting modalities, and deploy his forces rapidly to many trouble spots around the globe. That required breaking through traditional Navy silos and creating new, dynamic, and more responsive organizations. At the same time, he needed to recast the thinking and culture of the Navy to recognize the political and economic reality that the Navy had to become leaner and far more efficient.

Like the ship's captain he once was, Clark recognized that he needed to quickly change the course of the Navy and adapt it to a new set of conditions. In the process, he discovered that once he had it aligned, he would be able to leverage what we call "the Enterprise Effect," the ability to rapidly change organizational cultures and create virtual organizations that quickly respond to new challenges. In doing so, he achieved remarkable results. On his retirement, one admiral told us, "Vern Clark's transformative impact on the Navy was second only to that of nuclear power."

That story, like others you'll encounter in this book, is about alignment and realignment, the most powerful tool of organizational improvement we know of. Alignment is a condition in which the key elements of an organization—its people, strategy, customers, and processes—work in concert to serve the primary purpose of the enterprise: increasing value for stakeholders. For business organizations, that means growth and profit. For not-for-profit entities the outcome may be accomplishing the mission, and for a hospital it may be providing better patient care at lower cost. Whatever the enterprise or its goals, the degree to which those key elements are integrated and work in concert will determine how quickly and successfully it will fulfill it primary purpose.

Achieving alignment in an organization is analogous to landing an airplane. The pilot must sense and respond to interactive variables that change as the plane makes its approach. Many things are happening at once. Crosswinds affect the aircraft's orientation to the runway, requiring continual adjustments. Airspeed must be reduced with the aid of the flaps and throttle. As the plane descends along the glide path, the rate of descent and the pitch and yaw of the plane must be controlled. If the pilot manages these many interacting forces properly, the plane maintains alignment with the runway and the glide slope as it makes a smooth and successful touchdown.

Aligning a department or an entire organization requires a similar ongoing balancing act that involves sensing, setting direction, linking processes and systems, and making adjustments. If you fail to adjust, you'll drift off course. Overadjust and you'll lurch from one side of the intended course to another. When organizations find themselves hopelessly ineffective and out of touch with those they serve, the usual cause is past failures to make the corrections that would have kept them on course to achieving their goals.

Alignment has two dimensions: vertical and horizontal. The vertical dimension is concerned with strategy and the people we rely on daily to achieve it. To the trained eye, an aligned organization is easy to spot. People have a clear line of sight to what their customers require and to the organization's strategy for delighting them. They understand the organization's overarching purpose—its Main Thing—and how their work serves it. Strategy is not abstract but is broken down into practical activities that employees can engage with and are capable of performing well. The strategy is also the right one for delivering real value to customers. Business processes are designed with customer needs in mind and change with agility as those requirements evolve. Thanks to real-time measurement, management has its finger on every aspect of alignment. When misalignment is detected, management identifies its location and cause and rapidly restores alignment.

We can also identify aligned organizations by their results. Aligned organizations consistently deliver improvements in customer loyalty, customer satisfaction, employee retention, and shareholder returns because they are nimble and can adjust quickly to change.

An aligned organization is not a "one trick pony" that delivers a single business result: either profit or customer satisfaction or employee satisfaction. It can do it all. In that context, as a former Air Force pilot, George Labovitz is reminded of a fighter-bomber called the F-105. The Air Force called it the "Thunderchief." The pilots called it the "Thud." The manufacturer said it could fly far, could fly fast, and could carry a heavy bomb load. The pilots agreed. It could do all three things. "The trouble is", they said, "*it can't do all three things at the same time!*"

Organizations that successfully achieve alignment are nimble and respond quickly to change. They deliver measurable business results *simultaneously* in customer satisfaction, profitability, and employee satisfaction. They can do "all three things at the same time."

An organization with these characteristics is not a pipe dream. We've seen them in many types of enterprises: nonprofit hospitals, military commands, service companies, and manufacturers. Because everyone from the C-suite to the mail room is attuned to customers and strategy, the staff adjusts quickly to changes and to opportunities in the competitive environment; this is what we call *rapid* realignment. New or altered strategies are rolled out quickly. Business processes adapt and improve as customer needs change. Employees quickly engage with the new reality of the business.

Rapid realignment is an imperative that today's executives cannot ignore. Our Boston University friend and colleague, Professor Lloyd Baird says it very succinctly: "You folks don't have a choice. You can go for rapid realignment, or you can go out of business fast."

We began developing and applying alignment methods in the late 1980s as an extension of our company's quality management consulting work. What we learned became the basis of our book *The Power of Alignment* (Wiley, 1997). That small volume sold remarkably well and led to more consulting engagements in a variety of industries, and that, in turn resulted in further learning and refinements of our methods. Perhaps the most important thing we learned during those years was the importance of *rapid* realignment. As the pace of technological, competitive, and social change increases, organizations must develop the ability to realign rapidly.

Two technological developments of the last dozen or so years have also influenced our approach to alignment: social media and web-based measurement tools. Consider social media. We are in the middle of a paradigm shift in the way people communicate both inside and outside organizations. That shift, driven by new social media technologies, is altering internal and external relationships, business models, and the way we do work. It is dramatically changing the way we understand and engage with information and collaborate with customers. Harnessing these social media enhances our ability to realign quickly in a fast-changing world. Social media make it possible for companies to engage their employees and customers more fully in product development, obtain feedback on existing products and services, and more quickly align their work processes with customer requirements.

Social media can enable and foster this kind of "alignment communication." Besides getting understanding and engagement from employees, management can use it to get rapid feedback on implementation issues. It's fast and open, it invites collaboration, and it encourages people to align themselves. Marc Benioff, the founder of Salesforce.com, put it this way in a *New York Times* piece written by Tom Friedman: "There has never been a more important time to have all your ships sailing in the same direction. The power of social media is that it is easier than ever to both articulate, and reinforce, the vision and values that create and inspire alignment."[1]

At the same time, new software tools make it possible for the first time to measure alignment frequently, at low cost, and in real time. Using web-based measurement systems, management can identify areas of internal misalignment in any and all areas of operations. These web-based systems make it possible to answer questions such as these:

Do employees understand our strategy?

Do they see how their work fits in?

Are managers and supervisors listening to the people doing the work?

Is there a sense of urgency about reaching strategic goals?

Are the resources aligned effectively to accomplish the organization's goals?

What stands between us and our goals?

The Right Medicine for Today

Our work with for-profit and nonprofit organizations tells us that their leaders are wrestling with two big challenges: change and complexity. Today's leaders face substantial change on many fronts at once: globalization, technology advances, changes in the demographics and skill level of the workforce, and evolving customer requirements. At the same time, leaders of megaorganizations confront enormous complexity. They are trying to guide business units, subsidiaries, and acquired entities that make and sell very different things to very different customer groups. Many business cultures may be living under their broad umbrellas. These and other differences increase the complexity with which leaders must contend. Nonprofit entities are also struggling with high levels of complexity. Hospitals, for example, find themselves in a crosscurrent of new medical treatments, rising patient expectations, political pressures, partnerships with other institutions, and constricted funding.

What changes and complexities are roiling your organization and keeping you awake at night? Whatever they are, you must be able to *sense and respond* rapidly to them. The tools of alignment make that possible.

Since completing our previous book, we have learned from clients that the process of alignment is becoming more challenging than ever. Internal and external pressures require continuous and simultaneous realignment of the critical elements: strategy, customers, processes, and people. Hence, the title of this book is *Rapid Realignment*. We have also learned that culture determines whether change can happen quickly and successfully.

The problem of changing culture is surely familiar to every leader who must deal with mergers and acquisitions. Hence, we explain in this book how leaders can be cultural architects. The practice of realignment can help them better align their culture with business goals, and this book shows how that can be done.

Slow, Fast, Faster

As you will see in the cases that follow, leaders who have rapidly transformed their organizations have begun slowly. They took the time to listen to employees, customers, and other stakeholders. Before launching change efforts they used social media and web-based assessment technologies to gain insights into the current state of their organizations and their cultures. Without data and those insights, their efforts would have fallen into the Ready-Fire-Aim trap that results in frustration and failure. These cases demonstrate how knowledge and understanding provide a solid foundation for rapid realignment and high performance.

What's Ahead

The chapters that follow explain our concept of rapid realignment and offer practical methods for implementing it in any type of organization. Chapter 1 provides an overview of the alignment framework and its two axes: vertical and horizontal. This is the big picture. Chapters 2 and 3 consider the vertical axis and engaging employees: aligning people with strategy and with one another. Driving strategy down to those who do the work and getting them to buy into the strategy with energy and passion is one of the fundamental requirements of alignment. Many organizations fail miserably in this important task, and it shows: their leaders change strategy, but people keep on doing what they've done in the past. And those leaders ask themselves, Why isn't our new strategy working?

Chapter 4 moves to the horizontal axis that connects the many value-creating processes of an organization with its customers. Those processes should be informed by real customer needs and designed to give customers what they want the way they want it. Large enterprises usually have many specialized units. Those units often become "silos" of self-interest. Getting people to think beyond their narrow concerns and act in concert on behalf of customers is a tremendous challenge. Alignment tools provide the solution.

That wraps up our framework. Each subsequent chapter offers tools and insights you can use to rapidly align and realign your organization as you strive to attain competitive advantage in a fast-changing world.

Throughout this book you will find examples drawn from our many years of management consulting and will encounter some interesting people. We have had the privilege of working with many remarkable leaders who intuitively understood the power of alignment and used it to transform their organizations. These individuals have, over the years, shared their experiences and insights with us. We are indebted to them. They have taught us a great deal. Their examples of leadership and alignment inform every chapter of this book, and any organization of any size can benefit from them.

As you read this book you will encounter short case studies based on interviews and work with executives who have stepped up to the challenge of rapid realignment and succeeded. Those cases represent a broad spectrum of organizations, industries, and challenges, including the following:

- *Federal Express.* This is one of the best-aligned and best-led companies we have worked with. Under the guiding hand of founder/CEO Fred Smith and his executive team, FedEx has demonstrated the power of relentless customer focus and continuous measurement of critical success factors.

- *Quest Diagnostics.* Ken Freeman, now dean of the Boston University School of Management, shares his knowledge and experience when, as chief executive officer (CEO) of Quest Diagnostics, he led a dramatic and successful realignment of that company. He describes how he applied the principles of alignment to a number of other companies.

- *Navy Hospital at Camp Pendleton.* This military healthcare facility aimed for a huge increase in user satisfaction. Using alignment principles, it went from near the bottom of the Navy's healthcare facilities ratings to near the top.

- *Farmington Savings Bank.* Situated near Hartford, this Connecticut financial institution grew rapidly under the leadership of John Patrick, a new CEO who recognized the importance of engaging employees with the Main Thing of the business and its strategy. He started his realignment process at the top, with his board.

- *The Naval Aviation Enterprise (NAE).* U.S. naval aviation is one of the world's largest technical enterprises. It is composed of two huge organizations: one responsible for the acquisition and repair of aircraft and the other responsible for aircraft carriers and pilots. A high percentage of its aircraft were nonoperational, and wear and tear was taking a toll on the rest. The admirals in charge of the two silos overturned precedent and created a virtual, integrated organization called the Naval Aviation Enterprise. NAE achieved dramatic improvements in aircraft availability and returned billions of dollars in savings to the Navy. The enterprise leadership lessons in this case can be applied to any organization beset with a silo mentality.

- *Dana-Farber/Children's Hospital Pediatric Cancer Center.* Dana-Farber Cancer Institute is a world leader in cancer research and treatment. Children's Hospital Boston, situated in the same neighborhood, is the pediatric teaching hospital of the Harvard Medical School and a cutting-edge treatment center for young people. Each of these very different institutions had its own staff, facilities, budget, fund-raising apparatus, and agenda. Nevertheless, they formed a virtual organization to seamlessly bring young cancer patients the world's most advanced forms of treatment. To its "customers"—patients and their parents—the two hospitals are a single organization. Is your company involved in a joint venture? Is it struggling to align the capabilities of acquired entities with its own? Is it failing to capture the synergies that the dealmakers anticipated? If it is, the Dana-Farber/Children's Hospital story may provide insights for addressing your problems.

- *Naval Sea Systems Command (NAVSEA).* Measurement is a critical tool for achieving alignment. This case describes how NAVSEA applied a web-based system to obtain timely alignment measurement of every important function, making huge strides in alignment and command-wide performance in the process through a series of "hundred-day marches."

- *Wilhelmsen Lines.* When the entire senior executive team of one of Norway's largest shipping companies was killed in a plane crash, Ingar Skaug, the new CEO, had to deal with grief-stricken employees while realigning the strategic direction of the business and its culture. The steps he took are consistent with our slow-fast-faster approach to organizational change.

Let's move on to Chapter 1, where we introduce the alignment framework.

ONE

The Big Picture: The Alignment Framework

An overview of the framework

How the Main Thing fits in

Case example of the framework in action

The first challenge of alignment is to get everyone on the same page by understanding the organization in the same way. Every enterprise for which we have worked, whether industrial, government, or healthcare, here or abroad, has four major elements. Each has a strategy. Each employs people to execute the strategy. Each has customers. Each has processes for meeting the needs of those customers. The relationships between those four elements form our alignment framework, which helps people understand the *story of the business,* that is, the way the business works.

As shown in Figure 1.1, our framework has two axes: one vertical and one horizontal. The vertical axis links people with strategy; the horizontal axis connects business processes with customers. Both are animated by what we call the Main Thing: the ultimate purpose of the organization and the unifying concept to which every employee and every unit can contribute.

FIGURE 1 . 1
THE ALIGNMENT FRAMEWORK

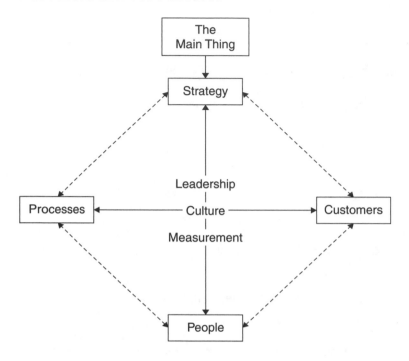

Vertical alignment describes a condition in which every employee can articulate the enterprise's strategy and explain how his or her daily work activities support that strategy. Horizontal alignment breaks through the boundaries that often separate companies from their customers. Employees in horizontally aligned organizations notice the linkages shown in the figure between strategy and customers, between people and customers, and so forth. Alignment between these elements is as important as alignment on the two axes. A strategy, for instance, that doesn't align or make sense for customers will undermine everything that the organization and its people attempt to do. The same thing can be said for strategy and processes. A brilliant strategy for addressing customer needs will do little good if the organization has not developed business processes that efficiently and effectively deliver the goods!

The four elements in our framework—strategy, people, processes, and customers—must be aligned and *re*aligned to achieve high performance. Accomplishing this requires mastery of two essential *competencies,* each of which we address in this book. These are the ability to do the following:

- *Rapidly deploy strategy.* We emphasis *rapid* because strategies in a fast-moving world must change periodically, and when strategies change, the people who implement them must quickly understand and get behind them. The processes that support strategy must also realign quickly; you cannot launch a new strategy today and wait a year or more for key business processes to catch up. This competency requires an understanding of the external market as well as the organization's internal culture.

- *Continuously improve the core processes that serve customers.* This alignment competency links the voice of the customer to continuous improvement. It requires a clear understanding of who the customers are, their current requirements, how well the organization is meeting their requirements, and who does it best. World-class companies have a common language and tool kit for continuous improvement. One of our clients told us that he can go from Seattle to Shanghai to Stockholm and know that every suggestion for improvement presented to him will be based on fact and a disciplined process for improvement.

Real-time performance measurement is an essential part of these competencies. Measurement indicates when and where misalignment is occurring. Measurement is so important in our framework that we will return to it often in this book. The chapter on rapid realignment (Chapter 8) explains how a web-based tool and employee participation can reveal points of misalignment at any level—down to the smallest department or activity. Armed with that knowledge, management can intervene when and where intervention is most needed.

The Main Thing

"The main thing is to keep the Main Thing the main thing!" We loved that expression when we first heard it from Jim Barksdale, then the chief operating officer (COO) of FedEx. That single sentence captures the greatest challenge facing managers today: keeping their people and the organization centered on what matters amid the crosscurrents of change. There are two aspects to that challenge. The first is to get everyone headed in the same direction with a shared purpose. The second is to integrate the resources and systems of the organization to achieve that overarching purpose: the Main Thing.

Every organization needs a Main Thing: a single powerful expression of what it hopes to accomplish. Growth and profits are surely the ultimate aim of every business organization, but they are outcomes of succeeding with the Main Thing.

In our experience, no organization captures the essence and importance of having a defining Main Thing better than FedEx, and no one personifies and articulates it better than its founder and chairman, Fred Smith. We first met him in the late 1980s, when we began helping that company implement Total Quality Management (TQM). At our initial meeting with the executive team in the Memphis headquarters, one of its members asked us what the team could expect to get from the company's sizable investment in TQM. Answering a question with a question, George asked, "What do you want back?" There was quick consensus about profit and customer satisfaction and retention and, after a brief discussion, employee satisfaction and retention. At that point, CEO Smith stopped the meeting, declaring, "Not at Federal Express!"

"We are in the service business," he continued. "How can we deliver world-class service without world-class people?" At FedEx, he said, "it must be people, service, profit, in that order!"

What we think is brilliant in this simple statement is that it teaches us that if we concentrate our efforts on recruiting and training the best people we can find, manage them effectively, and concentrate their efforts on delivering flawless service to customers, profit will follow.

Profit becomes the dependent variable, the reward for doing the first two things very, very well. Smith's adherence to staying aligned with the Main Thing of People-Service-Profit has guided the growth of FedEx and sustained its commitment to operational excellence.

Smith described to us his understanding of the Main Thing, which he refers to as the "theory of the business":

> Every successful business has, at its heart, a theory of the business—an underlying set of supporting objectives and a corporate philosophy that gives people a foundation on which to operate. Working inside that framework, they've got an idea of what we want them to do—to prioritize. We [at FedEx] have a very clear business mission and a business theory which is understood certainly by every member of the management team and probably by 90 percent of the workforce.

In our framework, the Main Thing is critically important. It is the end that strategy and human effort serve. We cannot achieve and maintain alignment without consensus and conviction about the Main Thing. Yet we are always amazed by how few people can articulate their organization's Main Thing. When we ask participants in workshops, "What's your Main Thing?" we see people digging into their wallets for the latest mission statement. Others look questioningly to the person sitting next to them. We wonder how these people can formulate a strategy or know how well they are doing if they cannot even state—or agree on—the ultimate purpose of their work.

Some people, however, can articulate their Main Thing without hesitation. Here are a few examples:

- At FedEx, as its CEO stated, the Main Thing is unambiguous: "People-Service-Profit."
- An official in charge of nutrition at the U.S. Department of Agriculture named her organization's Main Thing as "ending hunger in this country."

- An electrical utility executive explained his company's purpose crisply and clearly: "to be the power source of choice."
- The CEO of Connecticut's Farmington Bank told George that its Main Thing is to "drive economic development in central Connecticut."
- The U.S. Navy's huge Naval Aviation Enterprise, which supplies aircraft and trained crews to the fleet, has boiled its Main Thing down to a simple phrase: "aircraft and crews ready for tasking at lower cost."
- Boston's Port Authority, which has responsibility for bridges, airports, and harbor terminals, once described its Main Thing as "advancing Boston's pace of economic development."

Our good friend Claude Roessiger has long experience with luxury brand management. He likens our concept of the Main Thing to a strong brand. "A brand," he explained, "produces an emotional response and at the same time communicates to all how to behave." Your Main Thing should do the same.

What is the Main Thing for your organization? Can you articulate it clearly and concisely? Can your subordinates? In many organizations, people have no clear answer or will offer a confusing list of lofty goals. Others will describe a strategy. But a strategy is not the Main Thing; it is merely its servant. In some cases senior management defines the Main Thing one way and the people in the trenches define it in another. People or policies work at cross-purposes in these cases; one person is pulling when the other is pushing.

As you formulate a Main Thing for your organization, refer to the following guidelines:

- The Main Thing for the organization as a whole must be a common and unifying concept to which every unit can contribute.
- Each department and team must be able to see a direct relationship between what it does and this overarching goal.
- The Main Thing must be clear, easy to understand, consistent with the strategy of the organization, and actionable.

Alignment and high performance are achievable only when everyone can articulate the Main Thing and his or her role in serving it. It is easy for employees in big companies with functional departments to lose sight of what Fred Smith calls the theory of the business or to confuse it with preparing financial statements, creating marketing plans, writing software, or whatever. Employees need to see the larger purpose in their individual jobs and their connection to the Main Thing. That is why managers at every level—from top to bottom—must be concerned with alignment.

The Framework in Action

To better understand how the various elements of our alignment framework fit together, consider the case of Farmington Bank, located in Farmington, Connecticut. John Larrere, head of the leadership and talent practice at the Hay Group, introduced us to its CEO, John Patrick, Jr. Larrere thought this bank's story fit perfectly with our alignment framework, and he was right. The story touches each of alignment's key elements—the Main Thing, strategy, people, customers, and processes—and provides a glimpse of what an organization can accomplish when it gives each one its due.

John Patrick, Jr., came to the Farmington Savings Bank from Banknorth. There he grew an organization with six branches and $250 million in assets into a division with 84 branches and over $8 billion in assets. The lessons he learned there proved invaluable when he assumed the leadership of Farmington Savings Bank. He credits his success at Banknorth to his mentor, William Ryan, the CEO.

Farmington's Main Thing

The 160-year-old Farmington Savings Bank, situated not far from Hartford, Connecticut, was so much a fixture in its community that some of Patrick's peers saw his move as a relaxing cap to a successful career. As caretaker of a venerable old mutual savings bank, they speculated, the new CEO would become a pillar in the local business community and have lots of time for golf. But that wasn't how Patrick perceived his role. He was animated by a larger aspiration: to make the bank a driver of economic vitality in central Connecticut. That aspiration drove all that followed.

Strategy and People

As if to confirm that life is full of surprises, consider John Patrick's first week in his new job. Bear Stearns had just collapsed, and the entire U.S. banking system was trembling with fear. Was this the second coming of the Great Depression? Would the nation's banks tumble like dominoes?

Dramatic changes in the economy and the banking world took place in the weeks and months that followed, making the new CEO realize that Farmington Bank needed a new strategic direction and operating modality if it hoped to survive and prosper. But with the world of banking turned topsy-turvy, Patrick had to move and move fast.

Under the previous regime, the bank's strategic planning had been accomplished in concert with a banking industry consultant. The board would approve the plan, and business would proceed as before. Within a few weeks no one at the bank could find the strategic plan. Patrick changed this annual ritual. He believed that strategy had to begin at the board level and then work its way down through the company: from the board, through executive management and senior management, and finally to the employees, gaining buy-in on its journey. He believed that this process was fundamental to creating a culture in which everyone believed that it was *his or her* plan, not the consultant's, and had a part to play in it.

Gaining alignment at the very top, within the bank's small but dedicated board, was the first of Patrick's challenges. The postcrash world of banking would be much different from the one they had known. Competition would be fiercer, and the demands of new federal legislation would require the bank to have much more capital. To meet the new federal compliance requirements, Farmington had to limit growth in favor of building reserves or find other sources of capital. By Patrick's calculation, the bank needed a larger capital base in order to be a player—perhaps $1.5 billion in assets (from its current $900 million). Added assets and capital growth would shore up the bank's financial position and give it the funds it needed to modernize its information technology system, upgrade its facilities, expand the number of branch offices, and hire talented personnel. Since Farmington had added only about $10 million in new capital from operations in its best previous year, something had to change: perhaps an initial public offering (IPO) was in order. John Larrere's interviews with each board member indicated a lack of consensus about so bold a move.

The new CEO knew that the first step toward alignment would be to forge alignment within the board. Toward that end, he aimed to bring people face to face with the new reality. Everyone was proud of the bank's position in the community. They all believed that Farmington Savings Bank, founded in 1851, was widely known and loved in the community it served. That perception, however, was wide of the mark. A study commissioned by Patrick found that the bank had the second lowest name recognition in its marketplace. Furthermore, decades of penny-pinching on physical infrastructure had made the bank unappealing to younger customers, among whom Farmington Savings was perceived as "Grandma's bank."

Timely operating information and regular measurement of processes and results was another of the CEO's tactics for bringing reality to the board and other decision makers and changing the culture for the better. As Patrick saw it, establishing metrics and milestones would arm the board with information about corporate progress and serve as the basis for rewards and recognition. This in turn would create a healthy culture of accountability, responsibility, and action.

Employees and a new management team were important factors in the Farmington Bank's makeover. Several key managers had elected to retire, creating opportunities to bring in executives with whom the new CEO had worked before. Some brought expertise from outside the banking industry. A new chief financial officer joined the team in 2009. The new senior team also expanded to include managers from key areas that had been unrepresented. Among them were the head of retail banking, which contributed half of total revenues, and the bank's head of operations. The head of human resources (HR) also joined the team. "If you want to encourage accountability and responsibility," said Patrick, "the head of HR should be sitting right next to you. That person's doing the hiring."

HR followed through with performance-based rewards and recognition events. When those things were threatened by cash pinches, the annual Christmas party was sacrificed to keep rewards and recognition funded.

Processes and Customers

It was clear that the bank needed to retool its marketing image and customer connections. It created awareness by means of billboards placed strategically along the area's congested interstate highway and by sponsoring radio broadcasts from the local rush-hour traffic helicopter. Commuting residents of Farmington, going to and returning from work in nearby Hartford, were a captive audience with little else to see or listen to as they labored through bumper-to-bumper traffic. The bank also got closer to its customers through a number of new, attractively appointed branch offices. To make the bank even easier to do business with, operating hours were extended from closing at 3:30 p.m. to 7 p.m. and branches stayed open on Saturdays. Those extended hours soon accounted for 28 percent of the bank's business.

Equally important, the bank undertook process improvements aimed at enhancing its ability to deliver the quality, speed, and convenience that customers expected. Notable improvements followed. The time needed to open fully functioning new branches fell from three years to eight months. The loan approval process plummeted from as long as six months to two days for most applications. Those improvements were achieved by working across operations, IT, retail banking, and business banking and by recruiting branch management people with retail, not necessarily banking, experience.

Within three years, Patrick and his team had converted their quiet little community bank into a well-aligned financial powerhouse with plenty of muscle. It went from number 57 in Small Business Administration ending in Connecticut to number 2. Where once it could not generate a volume of mortgages on its own, Farmington Bank leaped to third place in Hartford County, behind the mortgage giants Bank of America and Wells Fargo. Most important, the bank achieved his goal of growing from $900 million to $1.7 billion in assets with 19 branches.

In mid–2011 the company launched a very successful IPO, raising over $170 million to capital, and converted Farmington from a mutual saving bank to a public, shareholder-owned financial institution. As Patrick told investors and the community, "Pursuing this path will ensure that Farmington Bank remains strong and continues to meet the needs of our customers and the community."

The bank's success was a tribute to the power of alignment and the affirmative, proactive leadership of its CEO and his team. Starting with the Main Thing, "being a driver of economic development for central Connecticut," they built a culture that focused on strategy, people, customers, and processes. John Larrere noted that Farmington Bank combined sound strategy development with earnest and determined execution. "Execution," he observed, "was enabled by close alignment among the board, executives, managers, and associates, who used similar data sets to develop and cascade a strategy around which they could commit and align." He also pointed to the energetic role of the CEO:

> John was the chief "energy" officer and cheerleader, promulgating what the various constituencies had agreed to. After that, executives, managers, supervisors, and associates picked up the banner and led the charge. John continued providing the metrics with which all—from tellers right through to the board and now to shareholders—could gauge progress.

What changes and complexities are roiling your organization and keeping you awake at night? Whatever they are, you must be able to sense and respond rapidly to them. The practice of alignment can help you do this, and we will explain how in the chapters that follow, beginning with a closer look at alignment between strategy and people.

Key Points on the Alignment Framework

- Vertical alignment describes a condition in which every employee can articulate the organization's strategy and explain how his or her daily activities support that strategy.
- Vertical alignment facilitates rapid deployment of new strategy.
- Horizontal alignment provides a strong connection between business processes and customers, breaking through the boundaries that often separate the two.
- Employees in horizontally aligned organizations understand customers and are always looking for better ways to serve them.
- The Main Thing is the ultimate purpose of the organization: the unifying concept to which every employee and every unit can contribute.
- Alignment requires consensus and conviction about the Main Thing of the business.
- Measurement allows management to detect and rapidly correct points of misalignment.

Things to Do

- Using the guidelines in this chapter, articulate in one sentence the Main Thing of your organization.
- With your Main Thing in mind, complete and score the alignment diagnostic in Appendix A. Where are the gaps between where you are now and where you ought to be?

TWO

From Strategic Intent to Tactical Action: Vertical Alignment

What vertically aligned organizations look like

Symptoms of misalignment

Using PDR to achieve vertical alignment

One company's experience

The vertical dimension of alignment connects organizational strategy with the people who must transform it into meaningful work and engages those people in that process. Vertical alignment is achieved when employees at every level understand what the organization is trying to accomplish, its strategy, and the way their work connects to it. Vertical alignment energizes people, gives them direction, and opens the door to innovation and greater employee engagement. It makes rapid strategy deployment possible.

Characteristics of Vertically Aligned Organizations

Vertically aligned organizations reveal themselves in the way people behave and interact relative to goals and strategy. Anyone at any level of a vertically aligned entity can articulate the story of the business.

Managers can delegate with confidence, knowing that their people understand what the business aims to accomplish and what makes it tick. Employees understand who their customers are and how the work they do supports the company's strategy. Managers trust their people to learn more about customers and to reflect what they learn in their everyday work. They can also count on employees to continuously improve processes for serving and delighting customers. Two indelible examples in our experience reveal the characteristics of vertical alignment: one from the military and the other from the private sector.

A Delightful Surprise

In late 2004, Admiral Vernon Clark, chief of U.S. naval operations (now retired), paid a visit to Naval Air Station North Island in southern California on San Diego Bay. He wondered how well people in that important facility understood and supported the goals he had been pushing. Clark's Main Thing for naval aviation was to greatly increase the number of combat-ready aircraft and do that at substantially reduced cost. Reliability and cycle time reduction were important mechanisms for reaching that goal. But were those goals getting through to people in the field? Were they taking those goals seriously? The admiral aimed to find out.

Clark's first stop at North Island was the maintenance line for F18s, the fleet's main fighter-attack aircraft. An officer there briefed him chapter and verse on the principles that his team was following to improve the efficiency and effectiveness of the maintenance line. Without prompting, that officer went on to explain how their increasing efficiency and effectiveness served the goal of more task-ready aircraft at a lower cost.

Clark wondered if he had been set up. What he heard sounded too good to be true. Had this officer been coached to tell him what he wanted to hear? Wary about being taken in, the admiral strolled off to another area of the maintenance line, where he selected a civilian employee at random and asked what he thought of the improvement program being followed on the line. That worker responded that for the first time he had the tools and authority he needed to improve the maintenance process. In the ensuing conversation, the man demonstrated that he understood the readiness/cost objective and how his daily activities were helping the Navy achieve it.

By this time, Admiral Clark's doubts about the maintenance center's alignment with his top-level goals had largely dissipated. His next encounter ended any lingering doubts. He was introduced to a petty officer in an intermediate-level maintenance shop who without hesitation gave him an overview of the process improvements they'd made and how those improvements had helped him and his crew focus on repairing the right things, at the right time, in the context of readiness and cost-effectiveness. This petty officer, a Six Sigma green belt, went on to describe how process improvement tools had allowed him to optimize space utilization and increase aircraft readiness at reduced cost.

Bingo! The admiral was delightfully surprised. Those people were aligned with the Main Thing.

The Examiner's Encounter

Vern Clark's experience echoes one described to us several years earlier by Jim Barksdale, then COO of FedEx. His story was related to FedEx's winning the Baldrige National Quality Award. At the post-award reception, the lead Baldrige examiner took Barksdale aside, saying, "Let me tell you the *real* reason you guys got this award."

That examiner, who lived in Seattle, Washington, had been given the job of handling Memphis-based FedEx's application for the Baldrige award. Before his trip to Memphis, he stopped at a FedEx drop-off kiosk in Seattle to send a large box of materials that he didn't want to carry on the plane. The kiosk was attended by a young uniformed employee. In the course of their conversation, the examiner made a number of important discoveries.

Without revealing his job as a quality examiner, he said to the young woman, "I understand that your company has applied for some kind of quality award."

"Yes, sir," she replied. "The Baldrige Award."

"What is that?" he asked.

"It's the most prestigious prize in the United States for quality," she replied.

"Have you been personally involved in improving quality?"

"Yes, sir," she said. "I'm a member of the quality action team." She went on to explain that team's function and structure and the things she and her teammates were doing to increase satisfaction for customers and reduce costs for FedEx.

With a little prodding, she went on to tell the examiner about FedEx's Main Thing—People-Service-Profit—and explained how her work at the kiosk advanced the company toward achieving those goals. "We believe," she continued, "that if we take good care of our people, they will provide the excellent customer service that produces profits for the company."

That encounter made a huge impression on the Baldrige examiner. As he later told Barksdale, "She answered every question I asked." If a frontline employee working half a continent away from headquarters was that much in tune with her company's objectives, FedEx must be doing something very right.

Like Admiral Clark, the Baldrige examiner had encountered clear evidence of vertical alignment: the superglue that engages employees with organizational strategy and the Main Thing of the business.

Take a moment to think about your organization. If someone like Admiral Clark or the Baldrige examiner dropped into one of your facilities, what would he or she find? Would managers and employees be able to identify the Main Thing of your business? Could they articulate company strategy and the part they play in it? Keep those questions in the back of your mind as you read on.

Symptoms of Vertical Misalignment

The most visible symptom of vertical *mis*alignment is disconnection between the goals and strategies of senior management and the many departments and individuals charged with execution. Strategy never gets down to the people who do the work and deal with customers, or employees feel no connection to or engagement with the strategy. As we like to say, strategy never gets below the neckline. In some companies, that neckline is very high. Consider this example. In one of our engagements we were in a conference room with 15 senior executives. We asked, "So what's your strategy?"

Silence.

The CEO popped up and said, "What's wrong with you people? Two months ago we had an offsite meeting to formulate our strategy. And we all agreed on it."

"Well," we asked the CEO, "what *is* your strategy?"

A befuddled look. He began looking through his briefcase. Frustrated, he ordered his assistant to go to his office and "bring me the plastic card with the strategy."

Does that story sound familiar?

Here are some of the typical symptoms and outcomes of vertical misalignment:

- The reward system doesn't encourage the right behaviors.
- There is little upward information flow.
- Individuals and departments work at cross-purposes.
- Work processes are optimized for implementing a past strategy, not the current one.
- Below the C-suite there is little passion for the strategy.
- Strategy execution is haphazard.

Disconnection between strategy and people has been documented in many studies. The Grolman Group, for example, found that only 15 percent of the CEOs surveyed believed that strategic changes are well implemented by their organizations. A 2011 report by Booz stated that 53 percent of personnel do not feel that their company strategy will lead to success. Robert S. Kaplan and David P. Norton, authors of *The Balanced Scorecard,* have estimated that only 1 in 10 companies implements its strategy effectively. As reported by the Duncan Group, 73 percent of employees don't believe that they are supporting organizational strategies in their daily work. If these studies paint an accurate picture, enormous human energy is being wasted—doing nothing to move organizations closer to their strategic goals.

The cause of misalignment can often be found in the way strategy is created and communicated. In many organizations strategy is created at the top with little or no input from the people tasked with implementation. Typically, senior management convenes at a fancy resort for two days of work, often with a facilitating consultant. Lots of PowerPoint presentations are made. The corporate staff reports the latest market and competitive research, and debate ensues. By the morning of day 3 the new strategy is determined and announced to all. The imagery of electing a new Pope springs to mind, with e-mails to all instead of the traditional white smoke. Then on to the golf course. There is little talk of implementation and minimal communication with the people in the trenches. Follow-up and review are practically nonexistent. As a result, a true understanding and appreciation of strategy seldom diffuses from the C-suite to the operating units. The result is predictable: though the strategy has changed, there is little change in how employees go about their business.

Senior managers spend a lot of time thinking and talking among themselves about strategy. For them it's top of mind. It is their creation. But for the people in the trenches, strategy doesn't naturally engage the mind or the emotions. And why should it? Chances are, they had no hand in creating or shaping it. No one takes the time to explain how the strategy will change their work or their lives (or their customers' lives) for the better. No one helps them understand how their day-to-day work with peers, subordinates, customers, and suppliers will contribute to the strategy's success and to a more secure work environment with better pay and benefits for them. No one takes the time to align rewards with strategy as it changes direction. The rewards system continues to encourage behaviors that may no longer be appropriate.

There's also a trust issue here. Waves of layoffs and wage freezes for employees (while executive salaries have gone up) have caused many lower-level employees to distrust their leaders. Therefore, when a new strategy or improvement initiative is announced, their first thoughts are "Will this be good for me?" and "Are they serious?" Or they may think, "Why should I knock myself out for them?" Leaders must establish trust before they ask employees to alter familiar work routines, and trust has to be earned. Leaders earn that trust when they listen, when they genuinely open themselves to feedback and to ideas, and when they give others a voice in decisions that will affect their lives at work.

A Method for Rapidly Deploying Strategy to Achieve Vertical Alignment

To achieve vertical alignment, top management must rapidly deploy strategy down to the levels where it will be implemented. Why rapidly? Because the longer it takes for everyone to get on the same page, the more likely it will be that one part of the organization will begin moving at cross-purposes to another.

To rapidly deploy strategy, you must do three things:

1. Articulate the strategy by using the Plan, Deploy, and Review (PDR) process.
2. Identify aspects of the culture that will either slow down or speed up the process.
3. Use social media as part of a "catch-ball" process to engage employees in discussions about the strategy and its execution.

We explain PDR and catch-ball in this chapter. Because of their importance, culture and social media merit separate chapters, which you will encounter later.

PDR

PDR is a repeating cycle of *planning, deployment,* and *review* (Figure 2.1). It is a simple but powerful tool for getting strategy out of the executive suite and into the minds and behaviors of everyone in the organization.

FIGURE 2. 1
THE PDR CYCLE

Planning

Planning encompasses the strategic and annual unit planning with which most readers are familiar. However, to be truly effective, planning should do the following:

- Originate in the Main Thing of the organization. The Main Thing might be the overarching purpose of the enterprise (e.g., "to provide state-of-the-art healthcare for seniors") or a singular initiative to improve performance in a key area (e.g., "to achieve the highest level of customer service in the industry").
- Include critical success factors (CSFs). CSFs should be quantifiable (e.g., "correctly filled on-time order deliveries").
- Challenge people with stretch goals (e.g., for a production team, "reduce line switch-over time by 40 percent").

- Specify the activities and tactics that people will use to implement the strategy and reach their stretch goals (e.g., for express delivery truck operators, "put all letters and packages in the bin in the order of delivery before leaving the depot").

These are, in fact, the essentials ingredients of planning. Figure 2.2 indicates schematically how planning would be applied to a three-unit organization, using what we call a *planning structure tree*. Here the Main Thing is the inspiration for the strategy.

Each unit has quantifiable CSFs that are linked directly to the strategy. For example, if the strategy is to achieve greater market penetration, one CFS of the production department might be "per unit production cost"; another might be "line turnover time." The same company's sales force CFS might be the "number of new accounts opened." Also, each unit has a unique set of *stretch goals*: challenging but achievable objectives that motivate employees to accomplish more than what they are required to do. Leave it to individual employees and teams to figure out how they will achieve those stretch goals.

FIGURE 2.2
PLANNING STRUCTURE TREE

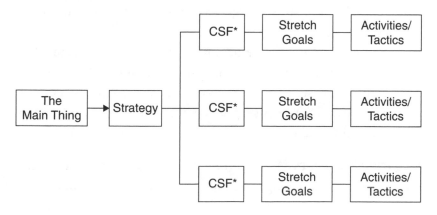

*CSF = Critical Success Factor

Deployment

The deployment part of PDR has one purpose: to bring strategy down to the day-to-day activities of employees. Strategy must be understood and embraced by everyone, and everyone must understand how what he or she does every day contributes to the strategy's success.

Four things can help you rapidly deploy your strategy: active employee participation, frequent communication, "catch-ball," and getting incentives right.

Active Employee Participation.   Successful strategy deployment begins in the planning phase with participation by the people who will implement the strategy. People are more likely to buy into a strategy or plan when they have a hand in formulating it. The notion, to quote Tennyson's poem about The Light Brigade, that "ours is not to reason why; ours is but to do or die" does not square with participative management, which gives people a feeling of ownership and a sense of accountability for results. Lack of participation creates a sense that the plan or strategy is being "imposed," which generates resistance. Let's face it, employees have much to contribute to planning and strategy formulation—more than most executives believe. Being closer to customers and daily competition they usually have a good feel for what will work and what will not. And remember, the Light Brigade's foolhardy charge was ordered by a guy who didn't know the territory.

Bring employees into the planning process. Bounce your ideas off the appropriate people as you develop plans and ask for feedback. That is one of the surest ways to build trust, overcome resistance to change, and avoid the nasty surprises that can occur when plans meet implementation realities.

Frequent Communication.   Communication is the second mechanism for deploying strategy from top to bottom. Good communication involves more than an e-mail to employees or a speech given in the cafeteria. Those things are useful but insufficient to the task. Your communication must both *explain* and *engage*, and the best way to do both is to meet with employee groups, lay out the strategy, explain its logic and how it will improve the prospects for the company and for them, and then engage employees in dialogue. Less is more here. The less talking you do, the more opportunities employees will have to speak. Dialogue should take place around the actual activities through which employees will put the new strategy to work. Be specific and concrete. Here are some examples:

Open five new retail stores in the Chicago area within the next 12 months

Develop and implement a plan to promote our new product through print media in eight key markets

Train six members of the department in Six Sigma quality methods

Reduce customer response time by 25 percent through process improvements

Employees will find dialogue on concrete activities such as these both useful and engaging, and this will help them align their daily work with strategic goals.

Repeat your communication about strategy at every opportunity. A story told once or twice will not stick. But if you keep repeating your message—and if that message is consistent—people will absorb it and act on it.

Lou Gerstner was a master of consistent, repetitive messaging. When he was the head of the card division at American Express, Gerstner launched a campaign to improve customer service quality, and he used every opportunity to get his message across to employee groups. Victor, who was doing work for American Express in those days, recalls how senior management used the first 30 to 40 minutes of every weekly staff meeting to ask people what they were doing to improve service quality for customers. This went on week after week. Gerstner, as we learned later, had learned the repetition trick from his own boss, American Express chairman Jim Robinson. As he said, "When the old man comes into your office every day for a year and says, 'Lou, what are you doing to improve customer service *today*?' you begin to think he's serious."

TELL 'EM AGAIN, ADMIRAL

Like most great leaders we've encountered, Vern Clark has his own story about the value of repetition. Shortly after being named chief of naval operations, he convened an "all flags" meeting of admirals at which he pitched his five key goals for the Navy, one of which was alignment. The speech was a big success. Shortly thereafter he gave the same speech to an assembly of the senior master chiefs, the Navy's highest-ranking enlisted personnel. Again, what he said was well received.

A year later, Clark was scheduled to address the chiefs again. But what should he talk about? Not wanting to bore his audience with the same speech, he turned to his own senior master chief for advice. "Tell 'em exactly what you told them last year, Admiral," he replied. "At least one-third of them missed last year's meeting. Another third won't remember what you told them. And the rest need to hear it again."

Catch-Ball. Another technique for getting people engaged with strategy is *catch-ball*, a component of the Japanese *hoshin* method for encouraging and ensuring alignment (see Figure 2.3).

In this technique, managers "toss" the strategy to employees, who are encouraged to understand it, reflect on its application to their work, suggest improvements, and then toss it back. Managers then digest what their employees have contributed, make some refinements of their own, and then toss the strategy "ball" back for another round. This back-and-forth, iterative process results in continuous improvements and a much better appreciation of the strategy and how it can be implemented successfully. Also, aspects of the strategy that might lead to implementation failure are usually discovered early and weeded out. (Social media provide new and extremely powerful ways to play catch-ball. See Chapter 6 for a discussion of this timely subject.)

FIGURE 2.3
CATCH-BALL

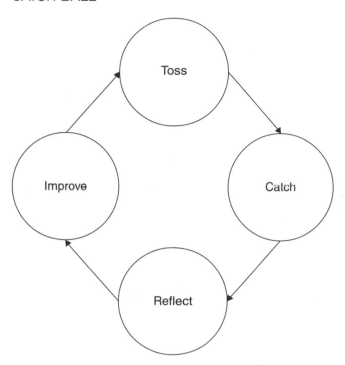

Getting Incentives Right.   Don't forget about incentives as you deploy strategy. Ask yourself, Do current incentives support the new strategy? Incentives should encourage people to do the right things. More specifically, they should align the self-interest of employees with company strategy. When incentives are properly configured, the invisible hand of self-interest motivates people to pay attention and work toward doing the things that matter.

Getting incentives right and preventing people from gaming the rewards system is far from easy. In the worst cases, people have incentives to do things that undermine top management's strategy. Steven Kerr's classic article "On the Folly of Rewarding A While Hoping for B" illustrated this point by using the example of the Vietnam War (among others). Anyone who served during that conflict will recall the policy of one-year tours. If a soldier could survive 365 days, he or she was home free. Counting down from 365 days began on day 1. At day 99, what the soldiers called "double-digit fidget" would begin.

Thus, although the country's strategy was to win the war, every soldier's incentive was to get through those 365 days, a goal that did not necessarily support the strategy. In contrast, World War II soldiers knew that they were in for the duration. Victory would be their ticket home; in this sense strategy and incentives were aligned. On the business front, Kerr reported similar misalignment. He noted that although top management hopes for long-term growth, it often rewards short-term gains; although it advocates teamwork, it rewards individual performance.[1] Is your organization rewarding A while hoping for B?

Review

The third element of our method, *review*, is every leader's tool for checking progress toward successful implementation. It is the critical element that draws the strategy down from the top to where it's executed. Review is too often overlooked. In *Star Trek: The Next Generation*, the commander would say, "Make it so," and the crew would dutifully implement his decision. End of story. Here on terra firma it's not that easy. A leader must personally and frequently check the progress of implementation. The leader must assure himself or herself that people understand the strategy and are acting on its behalf. He or she has to determine whether employees have the necessary resources and know-how at every stage of implementation. The leader must also confirm that the customer's voice is being heard and being responded to appropriately.

The Power of Review

We never fully appreciated the power of personal review until we witnessed Admiral Vern Clark, mentioned earlier, in action. As chief of naval operations, he personally involved himself in quarterly review sessions called Echelon 11 reviews with the leaders of the Navy's major systems commands. Those review sessions absorbed a great deal of his time but also stimulated a great deal of preparatory effort within those commands. At the end of one such review, Clark congratulated a group of admirals on the fine job they were doing in meeting goals and keeping up the pace of progress. And he announced that he looked forward to the next review in 60 days. Once he left the room, there were lots of high fives and backslaps and great relief that "the old man" hadn't found them lacking or forced anyone to walk the plank. That air of self-congratulation suddenly evaporated, however, when one admiral abruptly muttered, "Oh, S%$#@$!" The rest turned to stare quizzically at him, silently mouthing, "What?" He replied to their question by saying, "He's coming *back* in two months!" Yes, Admiral Clark would return for another review session in two months—and another two months after that. Those review sessions were his mechanism for keeping people focused on his goal and its implementation. Everyone in the room had performance goals to meet and milestones to achieve. Each knew that he or she would have to look the admiral in the eye and explain progress over the previous two months. That knowledge kept everyone focused and motivated. As Samuel Johnson put it, "Depend upon it, sir, when a man knows he is to be hanged in a fortnight, it concentrates his mind wonderfully."

Tips for Vertical Alignment

Bring implementers into the strategy-creation process to increase employee engagement.

Loosen the grip of command and control.

Create a practical system for measuring strategy-supporting activities.

Align employee incentives with strategy success.

Use your two most powerful tools for driving strategy from the top downward: repetition and review.

How One Company Got It Right

Our colleague Alan Burleson worked closely with a major U.S. cement manufacturer that had recently been acquired by one of the world's largest cement companies. The president of the U.S. entity was charged with integrating and realigning operations. For him the key goal was to "get everyone pointed in the same direction." His company, in our view, was a perfect candidate for the plan, deploy, and review phases of our methodology.

The planning phase began by giving the senior management team members a homework assignment before an offsite meeting. Burleson asked each executive to think five years into the future and imagine that the company had become wildly successful. With that rosy scenario in mind, each one was asked to write a one-page description of *what* the organization had accomplished and *how* it had done it.

The assignments were collected, copied, and distributed to each team member in advance of the meeting. Each member was asked to read what his or her colleagues had written and identify the factors most commonly cited for the company's great success: its *critical success factors*. Four factors stood out:

1. A realistic growth strategy
2. Employee satisfaction
3. Customer satisfaction
4. Measurement systems

Excellence in each of these, in the collective view of the company's leaders, accounted for the success they imagined for their enterprise.

At the offsite meeting, the team discussed those critical success factors and brainstormed a challenging but achievable goal for each one. For example, for the customer satisfaction factor, they reasoned that being "the long-term provider of choice for our customers" would get them there. They then began thinking about the areas in which they would have to focus to achieve those goals. Again, using the customer satisfaction success factor, they concluded that they would need to focus on their products, customer service, and customer relationships. If they did very well in each of those areas, customer satisfaction would follow.

The outcome of their working meeting was the draft of a planning guide to action similar to Table 2.1. As you can see in the table, the growth strategy goal—to increase revenues and profits—would be achieved by focusing on organic growth, growth into adjacent markets, and expansion into new markets, and the same process could be applied to the other CSFs. Each executive took this draft to his or her respective business unit for discussion, refinement, and buy-in.

Participation at the business unit level was deemed essential. Because the manufacturer's several units were highly decentralized and were facing different challenges, the executive team wanted to

TABLE 2.1
PLANNING GUIDE

Critical Success Factors	Goals	Where We Will Focus
Growth Strategy	Increase revenues and profits	• Organic growth • Growth into adjacent markets • Expansion into new markets
Employee Satisfaction	Attract and retain qualified people who are aligned with our goals and values	• Workplace climate • Performance rewards • Opportunities for personal growth
Customer Satisfaction	Supplier of choice for customers	• Our products • Customer service • Relationships
Measurement	An effective system for measuring performance against stated goals	• Information • Information sharing • Tracking progress

avoid a one-size-fits-all approach. Although the *critical success factors* and *goals* would be universal, the business units had discretion in the *areas of focus* that would move them toward those goals. The result was (1) greater buy-in by employees, (2) a planning guide that reflected the unique competitive challenge faced by each business unit, and (3) a process that got everyone moving in the same direction.

Business unit personnel were given the important job of translating the areas of focus into specific actions that people could incorporate into their daily work. These actions, for each area of focus, were structured as a series of statements describing the current state of operations and a final statement reflecting the successful operational practice that people aimed to achieve. Table 2.2 is from the company

TABLE 2.2
STEPS FOR CUSTOMER SATISFACTION

Goal: Supplier of choice for our customers
Area of focus: Our products

Steps to Excellence	Date	Actions Needed to Achieve the Next Higher Step
Our products are of poor or inconsistent quality		• Action plan for product improvement • Evaluation of the quality of our suppliers' materials • Team meeting to communicate quality goals
Our product are of average quality		• Upgrade process equipment as needed • Train employees in quality control • Reward quality gains • Review the action plan (above) weekly
Our products consistently meet or exceed customer expectations		**No actions needed once this level is reached**

planning guide for one of the critical success factors—customer satisfaction—and one of the three areas of focus within it: our products. The steps toward success in the product area—starting at the top—are shown in the left-hand column, descending from worst case to best. The actions required to achieve the next step—again from top to bottom—are in the right-hand column. Employees and their managers would use the "Where Are You Now?" section in the middle to indicate their current level of achievement over the time frame of planning and deployment. For example, if a team agreed that it was at the point where "We provide an average product at a competitive price," its members could see that getting better equipment, more training, and so on, would help them reach the next step: "We are a preferred supplier."

Every critical success factor and its areas of focus should have a unique set of steps to excellence and a set of associated actions. The goal for this cement manufacturer was for every unit to work its way through those many steps until it reached a point of excellence in each critical success factor—the point of alignment nirvana.

Each level of each business unit went through the same exercise, identifying where it was on the steps hierarchy and devising a set of actions—unique to its situation—that would carry it to a higher level of excellence. Needless to say, not every department took on all four CSFs. Rather, each identified an area of focus in which it could have a direct and positive impact. This "cascading" planning process went all the way down from the senior management team to frontline employees, effectively involving all personnel and aligning everyone with the company's goals. The resulting planning and deployment process was undertaken as a one-year project. Augmented with quarterly reviews by management, it greatly improved the company's performance over that time frame.

The president was so pleased with the result that PDR methodology became an ongoing activity. Like Admiral Clark, he began a series of skip-level reviews by asking, "Which of your critical success factors have you worked on, and what are the results?" During the five-year utilization of the methodology, his company consistently had the highest gross margin of the parent company's five international units.

Key Points on Vertical Alignment

- Vertical alignment ensures that the top and bottom of the organization are on the same page.
- Vertical alignment requires consistent and constant repetition of the strategy message.
- Review is the key driver of strategy deployment.

Things to Do

- Give the people who will implement your strategy opportunities to shape it.
- Communicate your strategy clearly and consistently.
- Help everyone at every level understand how he or she will contribute.
- Tell the strategy story again and again.

THREE

Energizing People: Employee Engagement

What we mean by employee engagement

Three techniques for engaging employees

Generating participation through force-field analysis

One leader's experience

People are one of the four elements in our alignment model. We have already explained how employees must understand company strategy, know how their day-to-day activities contribute to its success, and have a clear line of sight to customers. Strategy implementation is in their hands. This explanation, however, misses an essential aspect of people in our model. A colleague of ours put it to us this way: "Alignment of the two axes makes sense. It's logical. But there's something missing." After a bit of discussion he put his finger on the missing element: the human energy that springs from commitment and enthusiasm—what many academics and consultants call *employee engagement*.

He was right. As a system, our model for alignment is mechanically sound, like a good timepiece. But mechanical things don't do anything until we add energy. Even the finest timepiece, for example, needs energy from a wound-up spring or electric battery to tick off the seconds. The same is true of organizations; human energy is the force that makes them tick.

The higher the level of human energy in a business, the greater the level of activity and—assuming that people are doing the right things right—performance. We often remark to each other and to our colleagues that the energy level we see in client companies is a useful indicator of how well those companies are doing. Those which operate on a high-energy charge practically sparkle with enthusiasm and confidence. Their people are excited about what they're doing; they come in early and stay late without urging from management because they see their work as important. Those companies generally do well. In contrast, companies with low energy levels are dull plodders that fail to prosper.

Rapid realignment is possible only when employees are energized to move the organization in a new and better direction. Energizing the system from top to bottom is a key task of leadership. When that doesn't happen, organizational vitality winds down like a spring-driven clock. Athletic coaches have understood this for as long as there have been halftimes and locker rooms. If you've ever been an athlete, you know how much energy a great coach can put back into a team that is down on its luck. A great coach can pump up a team like a balloon, and the way he or she does that is by *engaging* players on an emotional level.

But rapid realignment requires energy that is focused, that drives continuous improvement and works to achieve the organization's purpose. This energy comes when an employee is engaged, so let's take a look at what engagement is all about.

ENGAGEMENT DEFINED

Employee engagement is a relative newcomer in the lexicon of organizational behavior. As two scholars who have studied it say, its meaning "is ambiguous among both academic researchers and among practitioners."[1] Some describe employee engagement as an amalgamation of personal commitment, loyalty, productivity, and ownership. Others describe it as the degree of an employee's emotional attachment to the job, to coworkers, and to the organization's goals or strategy. Though these definitions differ slightly, both capture important aspects of engagement. Keep in mind that engagement is qualitatively different from employee satisfaction and motivation.

Experience tell us that some individual employees and employee groups are more highly charged than others. One group is highly productive and intensely engaged with the strategy; it is more willing to go the extra mile that boosts profits and performance. These engaged people are consistently more productive, more profitable, safer, healthier, and, according to a study by the Corporate Leadership Council, 87 percent less likely to leave their employers. A second employee group is content to fulfill its duties and no more, and the members of a third group will do as little as needed to stay on the payroll. Do you see these three different groups in your organization?

The relative sizes of these groups—and their levels of responsibility—have an impact on organizational productivity and performance. In its workplace studies, Gallup, Inc., reports that the typical world-class company has a high percentage of engaged employees (67 percent), a smaller cadre of "not engaged" people (25 percent), and a tiny group (7 percent) of what it calls "actively disengaged" personnel. By comparison, in companies with average performance, only 33 percent are engaged, 49 percent are not engaged, and a disturbingly high 18 percent of employees are actively disengaged,[2] coasting along and picking up their paychecks, gaming the system, and sucking the energy out of everyone around them.

ENGAGED VERSUS ALIGNED

Engaged and aligned are two different things, and they don't always travel together. Research by the Corporate Executive Board has found that 40 percent of engaged employees do not align their behavior with organizational goals. Overall, it concludes that only 1 in 10 employees is both engaged and aligned with strategy. Clearly, many managers are failing to connect people with the strategies they are emotionally prepared to support with their daily work. This represents a huge lost opportunity.[3]

Looking at the engagement–performance connection from a different angle, the Hay Group has found that the positive effects of engagement vary with the complexity of employees' jobs. When they compared the performance of highly engaged employees with that of average employees, they found the following differences.[4]

- In low-complexity jobs, engaged employees produced 18 percent more value-added performance.
- In high-complexity jobs, engaged employees produced 48 percent more value-added performance.

Numbers like these support what most of us recognize from experience: the degree to which the employee population is engaged varies, and the greater the engagement, the greater its effectiveness and productivity. Thus, whatever you do to engage your people in their work and with the goals of the organization will pay big dividends.

Employee engagement and the participative management practices that go with it are not a panacea for every business problem, but we've seen them pay off time and again. For example, an employee engagement program at a Warner–Lambert plant led to a 21 percent increase in production and a 10 percent decrease in costs over a one-year period. A Canadian firm that engaged its employees in office space planning attributed a 15 percent productivity increase to that program.

How much could you gain by giving your employees opportunities to engage more fully in decisions, planning, process improvements, and day-to-day management? Some? A lot?

The Engaged Employee

In writing this chapter, we asked ourselves how best to describe the behaviors and traits of engaged employees. To find the answer, we went back to the definitions stated above. With those definitions in mind, we posit that engaged employees demonstrate

- Personal commitment
- Loyalty

- Above-average productivity
- A sense of ownership
- Emotional attachment to the job, to coworkers, and to the organization's goals or strategy

For us, no category of worker fits this description better than the entrepreneur. Entrepreneurs exhibit the kind of engagement we'd like to see in every employee. Whereas most people check in at nine and check out at five (with plenty of self-indulgent web surfing in between), the entrepreneur is "on" through most waking hours. Nothing commands his or her attention more than the progress and success of the business. Pulling together the best team, finding enough cash to meet payroll, solving problems, knocking on the doors of potential customers—these are the things that occupy the entrepreneur's thoughts and actions more than 12 hours each day.

For most entrepreneurs, business needs trump personal priorities. As a successful entrepreneur told one of our colleagues: "My friends have all learned to ski and play golf; I learned neither because I've been so tied up with this company. My wife and I had to reschedule our wedding three times because of business needs. And ten years later, we still haven't taken a honeymoon."

Now, that's engagement—on steroids!

Indeed, entrepreneurs represent an extreme level of engagement. But they aren't gluttons for punishment; they simply enjoy what they do at work. They willingly defer other interests because what they do every day at work is so personally satisfying. Equally important, their personal success and the success of their businesses are perfectly aligned.

If entrepreneurs are this engaged, it stands to reason that organizations can achieve high levels of employee engagement if they can get their people to think and behave like entrepreneurs. True, not every employee is wired to think and behave like an entrepreneur. Many or most find their greatest personal satisfactions outside the organization: in family life, hobbies, community work, and so forth. But even these employees will become more engaged and more entrepreneurial and *give more* of themselves when their leaders create the right conditions.

How Leaders Encourage Engagement

If you agree that engaged employees improve results, you're probably wondering what you can do to make it happen. We recommend that you do three things: listen, create a common purpose, and give people greater ownership of their work. Let's consider them in order.

Listen

Leaders should realize that they don't have all the answers and that their subordinates usually know more about their jobs than they do. Therefore, if you want to improve work processes, ask the people who have been involved in those processes day after day. The mere act of listening engages people. This lesson was brought home to us by a letter to the editor we spotted one day in the *Los Angeles Times*. The writer identified himself as a 16-year veteran autoworker. "A worker who performs a certain task 320 times a day, five days a week, for 16 years knows more about that job than anyone else," he wrote. "Yet," he continued, "in 16 years I had never been consulted or ever seen any other assembly line worker consulted on how to improve that job quantitatively or qualitatively."

That autoworker's experience is not unique. In seeking answers to problems, it's easy to overlook the expert knowledge that's under our noses. Desperate for answers, companies will pay huge fees to outside consultants but fail to listen to the expert consultants on their payrolls. One such case in our experience involved an industrial air-conditioning manufacturer that was having operational problems and losing both market share and profitability. This company had facilities all over the United States. In an attempt to revive its fortunes, the company's CEO engaged the consulting firm in Boston that George Labovitz was working for at the time. Before sending George and his team on a fact-finding blitz, the CEO suggested that they stop in Phoenix, Arizona, because, as he put it, "We have a bright young man there."

After spending almost two weeks on the road, visiting suppliers, customers, competitors, and employees, George and his team felt that they understood what was causing most of the company's problems and had generated a list of recommendations for senior management.

Believing that he had everything he needed, George did not want to stop in Phoenix on his way home from the West Coast. In deference to the CEO, however, he arranged to meet the "bright young man" in a Phoenix airport coffee shop. There, after the usual pleasantries, George invited the young manager to tell him what was wrong with the Phoenix-area operations. "I don't want to talk about Phoenix," the manager countered. "I want to tell you what's wrong with the *entire* company!" Writing on a paper napkin he grabbed from the counter, the manager systematically listed his company's problems, their causes, and his suggested remedies. As he wrote, George realized that the napkin replicated the lengthy consulting report he and his team had drafted the night before, which was now in George's briefcase. But this manager wasn't finished; he went on to list another three or four problems that George and his consulting team had failed to uncover.

Sitting there at the café counter, George realized that he was looking at a $70,000 napkin: the amount he would be billing the company CEO for the project. "Have you told anyone in the company what you've just told me?" George asked.

"Yes!" he replied. "Eighteen months ago I sent senior management a memo with this same information. They never responded. Six months ago, I was at the sales meeting in New York and said the same thing." He went on to say that during those 18 months his company lost hundreds of thousands of dollars and a number of key customers. This young man was, to cite the motto of Dartmouth College: *vox clamantis in deserto*, a voice crying out in the wilderness.

Sadly, we've encountered other versions of this $70,000 napkin case before and since in a variety of industries. Each could have been avoided if someone had listened to the voices of people closest to the problem. Managers and employees want to participate in and influence the design of processes and systems that affect them. They want to make things better. And they usually do that when given opportunities to engage and share what they know.

Create a Common Purpose

Help people understand what must be accomplished, why their work is worthwhile, and how they can accomplish their goals. We recommend the following:

1. Keep people continuously connected to the environment in which they operate. They must understand what is at stake.
2. Help people think holistically. People can't make good decisions if they cannot see the big picture.
3. Always keep people connected to the Main Thing of the entire enterprise.
4. Reward and recognize people for working toward the Main Thing.
5. Use the review process to carry the message to employees.
6. Create opportunities for people to communicate and interact.

Give People Greater Ownership of Their Work

Many readers are probably familiar with Frederick Taylor and the school of scientific management he established early in the twentieth century. Taylor was one of the first people to analyze industrial work by using time and motion studies. His goal was to increase productivity by finding and applying a set of most efficient steps, or routines, to any job. Nonmanagerial employees in the world of Taylorism were cogs in the machinery of production and were told to follow carefully developed scripts without deviation. They were told to "do" and leave the thinking to their bosses. The predictable result was widespread employee alienation from work and what Adam Smith referred to as "torpor of the mind." Coupled with meager pay and dangerous conditions, that alienation produced labor strife and an "us versus them" hostility that divided workers and management and often led to violence.

Whether scientific management's extreme level of control made sense in the workplace of a hundred years ago is hard to know. However, it has little to offer the modern world of knowledge work in which creativity, innovation, and continuous improvement are the essential virtues. We nurture those values when we give employees a sense of ownership and control over what they do every day. You can impart that sense of ownership by demonstrating trust, replacing the stick with the carrot, broadening the scope of jobs, and giving people more opportunities for self-management. It's not rocket science: people are more engaged and perform better when they feel and act like owners.

WHO WASHES A RENTED CAR?

U.S. Air Force General Bill Creech, who transformed and realigned the poorly performing Tactical Air Command before its success in the Gulf War, used an amusing story to underscore the power of giving people more control and accountability for their work.

In *The Five Pillars of TQM*, Creech describes his philosophy of decentralization and pushing responsibility as far down as possible in the organization. He also describes how he changed the centralized maintenance function and assigned a crew chief to each airplane, giving that person responsibility for its performance. He even insisted that the name of the crew chief be stenciled on the fuselage alongside the pilot's name. Creech discussed the changes with the crew chiefs and asked what they thought. He knew he had made the right call when one of the chiefs asked, "General, have you ever washed a rental car?" The reliability of aircraft skyrocketed.

Good bosses understand the value of giving subordinates a long leash. Over the years, we have asked thousands of managers and workers to think of the best boss they ever had. We then ask: "What did that person do to qualify as your best boss?" We almost always get the same responses:

My best boss listened!
My best boss backed me up.

My best boss trusted me and respected me.

My best boss gave me feedback.

My best boss left me alone.

When asked, "Did you work hard for your best boss? Come in early, stay late?" The response was always an enthusiastic "Yes." Those best boss behaviors are the building blocks of participative management. Participative management is the foundation of the quality and process improvement programs we'll discuss in Chapter 5.

Participative managers invite people to influence the design and implementation of systems and processes that affect them. The operative word is *influence,* not *vote* or *dictate.* When management invites participation, it generates employee motivation and provides an opportunity for employees to apply their job expertise to accomplishing organizational goals. The resulting employee engagement benefits everyone.

When should you consider using a participative management approach? We suggest the most appropriate situations times are the following:

- You don't know the answer.
- You want input and buy-in.
- You are managing change.

Over the years, our company, ODI, has trained thousands of managers in participative management techniques. They range from asking for input to more structured approaches such as force-field analysis. Here's a simple one. In a *Wall Street Journal* article that George wrote on the value of wandering around, he described how Bill Marriott would "let people influence" by dropping in unannounced at his hotels. Every visit began in the kitchen, where Marriott asked the staff for ideas on improving operations.

Another client, a steel executive, took an afternoon walk around of his mill every Tuesday afternoon. He would ask every employee he encountered this question: "What's getting in the way of our making the best damn steel in the world?" Workers soon came to expect this executive on Tuesday afternoons and would line up to answer his question. Because he listened—and acted—that leader's mill became the only U.S. specialty steel company that could compete successfully against the Japanese.

Force-Field Analysis

Managing by walking around is a simple way to invite employee participation; in contrast, force-field analysis is a more structured and sophisticated approach. We have used it many times with very good results. In a nutshell, force-field analysis is a technique for identifying the *driving forces* that compel us toward an important goal and the *restraining forces* that impede our progress. The result of these combined forces is a form of equilibrium. For example, an aircraft at altitude is suspended between the upward force of lift and the downward force of drag. We see something comparable in business with respect to levels of output, profits, error rates, and so forth. To reach a better level, we need to alter the contending forces.

Force-field analysis involves three steps:

1. Identify and label your present state and the desired outcome in quantifiable terms.
2. Brainstorm the driving and restraining forces.
3. Design a plan to remove or weaken the restraining forces and strengthen the driving forces. That plan should list the events that must occur, provide a timetable of events, and specify the names of the people who can contribute.

Let's consider a hypothetical example of force-field analysis:

A production manager has gathered his entire team in a conference room to discuss the machine downtime that has been frustrating everyone. These employees have a natural interest in the problem of downtime because piecework bonuses are part of their compensation. Everyone in the room is eager to address the problem.

"We can tame this beast if we put our minds to it and work together," the manager tells them. "In that spirit, I'd like to challenge this entire group with a goal that will make each of us stretch: a 40 percent reduction in machine downtime. And because you're closer to the problem than anyone else, I want you to tell me how we can do it."

To organize their ideas, the manager went to the whiteboard and at the top wrote the goal in capital letters: 40% DOWNTIME REDUCTION. Beneath that goal he created two columns, one labeled "Driving Forces" and the other labeled "Restraining Forces" (Figure 3.1). The vertical line between the two columns represents the current state. He then went around the room, asking each person, "What is compelling us toward that goal, and what is standing in our way."

FIGURE 3. 1
FORCE-FIELD CHART 1

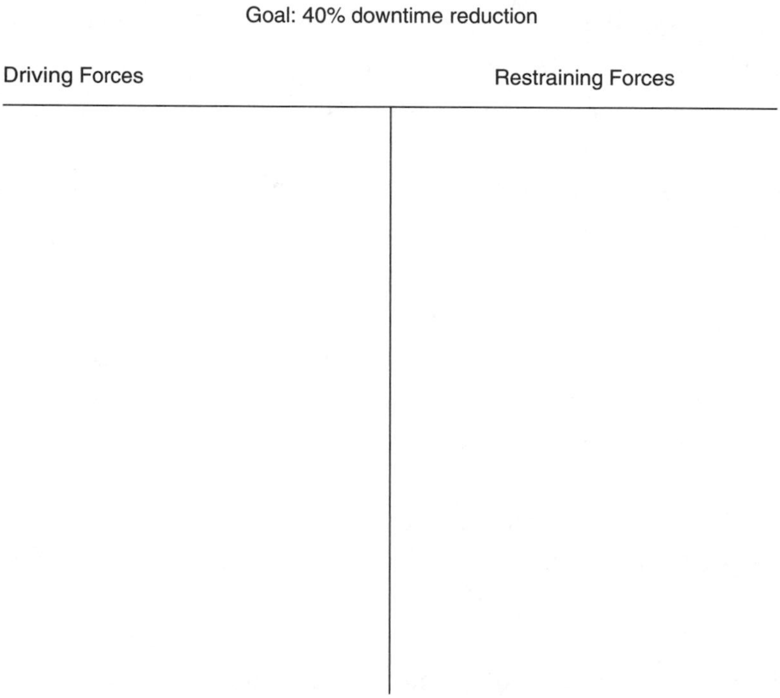

Goal: 40% downtime reduction

Driving Forces   Restraining Forces

The people in the room went on to brainstorm lots of ideas. Though a few had no ideas and passed, most had an idea or two to offer. Within 20 minutes, the manager had filled the force-field chart with many driving and restraining forces (Figure 3.2).

The manager had tapped the accumulated insights and know-how of the group. That was a good start, but to capture the full benefits of this technique, he and his people had to move from analysis to action by doing the following:

1. Eliminating the forces (driving and restraining) over which the participants had little control
2. Determining which driving forces could be strengthened and how

FIGURE 3.2
FIELD-FORCE CHART 2

Goal: 40% downtime reduction

Driving Forces	Restraining Forces
Competitors are pricing us out of the market.	Workers are not using a disciplined Improvement method.
Local management is under pressure from corporate. A new training system is being implemented.	Shifts are not cooperating in maintenance.
Layoffs will occur if line performance does not improve.	Too little time to train new employees
New IT system	Replacement parts take 7–10 days to obtain

3. Determining which restraining forces could be weakened or eliminated and how

4. Designing a prioritized action plan for steps 2 and 3, including timetables and personal accountability

One Leader's Experience

Our goal in this chapter was to help you recognize the contribution that engaged and energized employees make to organizational alignment, and we've offered some practical tips for gaining engagement. Let's cap the discussion with a profile of a man who has done it successfully and often.

One of the people we greatly admire for his ability to engage and align people in a common effort is Ken Freeman. Ken had an illustrious business career before becoming dean of the School of Management at Boston University, initially at Corning, where he was involved in several turnaround situations, and later at KKR, a leading private equity firm, where he did more of the same. When we asked if he could relate to our concept of alignment, he said, "Absolutely! In my own way I've tried to drive the power of alignment in the many turnarounds I've led. The biggest problem I encountered in each circumstance was that each organization didn't have aligned and engaged people."

In his experience, four things are required for success in business: (1) a plan that is straightforward and understandable, (2) effective execution of the plan, (3) flexibility, with a willingness to adapt to changes in the competitive environment, and, most important, (4) talented, engaged, and aligned people.

Ken shared with us his method for assessing how well or poorly an organization is aligned.

> I start at the top, asking, "How well aligned is the senior leadership with the goals of the business?" If top managers are only interested in short-term results, pumping up the stock price so that they can cash in and get rich, they won't be able to create sustainable shareholder value. I also establish open and transparent communication with all

employees on the various aspects of the business. If we successfully engage and satisfy our employees, we'll have engaged and satisfied customers; and if our customers are engaged and satisfied, then our owners will be happy; and if our owners are happy, some of that happiness will flow back to employees in the form of new opportunities, financial rewards, and other benefits.

Freeman's third alignment tool, beginning with the leadership and spreading throughout the organization, is to engage people in understanding the organization's position relative to its competitors on an ongoing basis. He has identified five possible performance stages for any business: bleeding, stable, gradually improving, rapidly improving, and out of touch with reality. He asks people the question, in terms of those five stages, "Where are we today?" He notes that companies in the out of touch stage are really bleeding but as a result of internal hubris or ignorance don't realize it. He cites IBM before Lou Gerstner's arrival as an example of a company that was out of touch.

In turnaround situations, he found initial differences in responses to his "Where are we?" question among senior leaders:

Opinions were often miles apart—a clear sign of misalignment starting at the top. Some executives thought the company was rapidly improving while others on the same management team maintained that they were bleeding. When the senior management team—the people responsible for driving alignment—is divided in their answers, you know that there are big problems throughout the organization.

Another clue to the state of alignment for Freeman is how well or poorly people understand the values and vision of the enterprise and the associated strategic goals:

In every turnaround situation I've encountered people would tell me, "I don't understand what my job is. I don't know how I fit in. I don't even know what our company's strategy is." Leaders must provide fellow employees with the context for doing their jobs: here's where we are; here's where we're going; this is our compelling vision of the future; and these are the first steps we will take together—as a team—on the journey. And most important, here is where you fit in.

Freeman uses what he calls a "plan-on-a-page," a simple but effective device introduced to him years ago by a Japanese colleague, to get this essential information across. Here's how it works. A single piece of paper (see Table 3.1 for an example from Ken's plan for Boston University School of Management) describes the organization's values, its vision, strategic goals in support of the vision to be achieved in the next 12 to 18 months, and specific significant actions required to achieve each goal. Performance metrics are used to monitor the progress of each action. Employees and leaders have a voice in developing the plan-on-a-page. Freeman then uses the plan to communicate with and engage employees and managers on an ongoing basis, literally ensuring that everyone is on the same page.

TABLE 3.1 PLAN-ON-A-PAGE FOR BOSTON UNIVERSITY SCHOOL OF MANAGEMENT	
Our values	Integrity, innovation, collaboration, accountability, leadership, respect
Our vision	Create value for the world through research and teaching
Key strategic goals	Enhance the student experience
	Broaden faculty contribution
	Develop an innovative curriculum and sector presence
	Build alumni engagement
	Develop and manage resources effectively
Key goal-supporting activities	Example: for "Enhance the student experience"
	• Foster world-class career services
	• Improve student service processes
	• Faculty advising process
Key metrics	• Student satisfaction scores
	• Number of faculty hires
	• Percentage and amount of alumni giving
	• Graduates' employment placement percentage

During his days as a turnaround leader, Freeman made heavy use of small group meetings, including skip-level sessions, to listen to and learn from managers and employees and provide an update on company performance. These were companies in significant trouble, with no unanimity on the "Where are we?" question. By being patient, open-minded, and welcoming of other viewpoints, Freeman succeeded in achieving both engagement and alignment, which served as the fuel for driving performance improvement.

"You get alignment," Ken Freeman says, "by finding the heart, the passion, and the common ground; by being transparent and sharing what's going on; and by creating an environment where people know where the company is headed, feel they are an important part of the team, and have the appropriate tools to do the job well."

Key Points on Employee Engagement

- Rapid realignment is possible only when employees are engaged with strategy and energized to make it succeed.
- Engaged employees demonstrate many entrepreneurial traits, including personal commitment, above-average productivity, a sense of ownership, and an emotional attachment to their jobs and to organizational goals.
- Leaders foster engagement when they listen to their employees, create a common purpose, and give people greater ownership of their work.

Things to Do

- Identify three opportunities you have this week to create a greater sense of common purpose among your subordinates.
- To what extent do your people own their work? Name two areas in which you could delegate greater discretion or decision-making authority to them.

FOUR

Getting to "Wow!": Horizontal Alignment

The characteristics of horizontally aligned companies

Catch-up and opportunity gaps

Getting horizontal alignment right

The price of misalignment

A case example of success

Just as alignment in the vertical axis ensures that strategy is embraced by employees and reflected in their day-to-day activities, horizontal alignment assures that customers' needs and concerns become part of the organization's thinking, planning, and employee behavior. Alignment on this axis integrates systems and processes with the needs of customers. It is every company's best assurance that its actions will delight customers and build the bonds of loyalty that produce growth and profitability. As with the vertical axis, alignment on the horizontal axis has an important precondition: alignment at the top. A high level of integration of systems and processes with the needs of customers will not be achieved if members of the senior team are divided by personal ambition or put the interests of their functions ahead of the enterprise's interests. Even though they may disagree on many things, they must be of one mind on how they will please customers.

The horizontal dimension of alignment connects customers with the business processes that serve them. It provides a clear channel between customer requirements and the way the enterprise works from day to day. Too often the customer voice coming through that channel is drowned out by internal chatter from reorganization work, turf battles, or a "this is the way we do things" culture. Horizontal alignment blasts through the chatter and hardwires the enterprise and its employees to what customers truly care about.

The voice of the customer in turn informs strategy, engages employees, and opens the door to new and attractive business opportunities. Consider FedEx, an exceptionally aligned enterprise. FedEx was initially in the next-day delivery business and was making tons of money, but as CEO Fred Smith told us, customers gave his company the idea for another business: low-cost ground delivery. Although customers valued FedEx's premium next-day service with real-time tracking, they had other shipment needs that were less time-critical and for which they were not willing to pay express delivery prices. Smith and his colleagues responded to that need with a new operating unit: FedEx Ground, an efficient low-cost and day-certain business-to-business and residential delivery service for packages weighing up to 150 pounds.

How horizontally aligned is your organization? Before your read further, try to answer the following questions, which are designed to reveal the extent of horizontal alignment:

- For each service your organization provides, is there an agreed-upon, prioritized list of what customers care about?
- When customers register complaints, are those complaints communicated to your people?
- Are your strategies reviewed periodically to ensure that key customer needs are satisfied?
- Are your processes evaluated regularly to ensure that they contribute to customer satisfaction?

What do your answers reveal about horizontal alignment in your organization?

Characteristics of Horizontally Aligned Organizations

Horizontally aligned organizations have the following characteristics:

- They understand what customers want and how they prefer to be served. And they base their strategies on that knowledge.
- Employees have access to customer information and are able to respond to it.
- Work processes are designed to deliver what both internal and external customers want the way they want it; they can change rapidly as customer requirements change.
- Process capabilities meet and try to exceed customer requirements.

Let's elaborate on these characteristics and consider some examples of effective practice.

Understanding What Customers Want

Horizontally aligned companies are information-driven. They have effective methods for gathering relevant and reliable information along both directions on the horizontal axis, that is, the information that comes from the outside (customers, competitors, suppliers) and internal information about the performance of their own customer-serving processes. Just as important, employees have access to that information and are empowered to act on it.

Employees respond quickly to changes in customer requirements. They also use customer feedback as an indicator for how well they are performing. For example, if product warranty claims or late deliveries increase, they look for the root cause. They have tools and methods for this purpose and are trained in their use. When they find the source of the problem, they fix the business process behind it.

Regular listening and responding to customers is a must for horizontal alignment. HCA Corporation surveys 125,000 patients every quarter. Patient responses are clustered into themes that represent the critical processes that the company targets for improvement. Some enterprises take matters a step further. FedEx surveys its customers every day because it thinks of itself as a 24-hour business.

LEARNING FROM LEAD USERS

One way to get out ahead of customer requirements is to spend time with users whose requirements for one reason or another far exceed those of today's marketplace. For example, a manufacturer of consumer automotive braking systems might look to the brakes developed by race car teams or jet aircraft makers for ideas on improving its current products. Because of their more demanding requirements, those lead users must often create their own products—they simply cannot find them in the marketplace. More typically, they modify or improve off-the-shelf products to meet their higher performance needs.

MIT's Eric von Hippel did the pioneering work in the field of lead-user innovation. His research found that users in some industries were the source of the greatest innovation—not the manufacturers or suppliers who served them. For example, he credited users of scientific instruments with 77 percent of instrument-related innovations as opposed to a mere 23 percent contributed by instrument manufacturers.[1]

In most cases, lead-user innovators have no proprietary interest in their inventions. They are glad to share what they've learned with whichever manufacturers or suppliers will provide them with the high-performance items they desperately need. Thus, enterprises that want to stay ahead of or anticipate customer requirements can learn a great deal by spending time with creative and demanding lead users.

Internal Customers and Suppliers

Everything we've said so far about customers has implied external customers. Yet the fact remains that most of us are internal customers of other employees and at the same time suppliers to others. In fact, most of us are part of a chain of internal customers and suppliers that ultimately extends beyond the boundaries of the organization to external customers. At IBM, the notion of internal customers dates back to the "basic beliefs" articulated by the company's founder, Thomas Watson. Among those beliefs is that the objective is "to meet the needs of your customer, and your 'customer' is whomever your work moves to next."

Consider a chain of suppliers and customers in which research and development (R&D) is a supplier to its customer: engineering. Engineering in turn supplies its customer, manufacturing, and so on, until the manufactured product is sold to an external customer. Even after the product has passed through distribution to the external customer, that customer probably is acting as a supplier to someone else—perhaps an original equipment manufacturer further along the value chain. Thus, most of us play dual roles as suppliers and as customers, as described in Figure 4.1 on page 66. In fact, work can be thought of as a process in which we, as customers, receive *inputs* (e.g., components), *add value* (e.g., through component assembly), and then pass along *outputs* (e.g., assembled units) to our own customers, who are either inside or outside the organization. Customer needs in this value-adding chain are best satisfied when every supplier in the chain puts them above his or her own needs.

Sales people often have the greatest problem in recognizing the needs of internal customers. Being totally focused on external customers, they often forget how they can be the eyes and ears of product development, logistics, and other internal functions. What they know about competitors and the needs of external customers could help those internal functions perform much better.

GEORGE'S THREE QUESTIONS

George wrote Labovitz a piece for the *Wall Street Journal* titled "Keeping Your Internal Customers Satisfied." In it he suggested that internal suppliers should always ask their internal customers three basic questions:

1. What do you need from me?
2. What do you do with my output?
3. Are there gaps between what you need and what you get?

(Continued on page 67)

FIGURE 4.1
MOST PEOPLE ARE SUPPLIERS *AND* CUSTOMERS IN A CHAIN OF VALUE CREATION

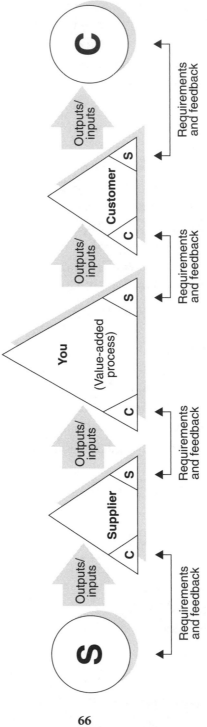

The day after the article appeared, he received a call from a manager in charge of 700 engineers at one of the world's largest computer companies. She explained that none of those engineers dealt with external customers. All of their customers were internal. "When I read your article," she said, "it reminded me of what happens when electrons flow through a wire." Labovitz, an organizational psychologist by training, confessed that he didn't have a clue about how electrons flow through wires, and so she explained: "When electrons flow through a wire, they lose energy at each connection." To her, the supplier-customer connection was a clear analogy. "If you can reduce the loss at each connection by asking your three questions, quality and productivity have to go up at the other end!"

Each supplier-customer interaction represents an opportunity for the supplier to learn more about his or her customer's requirements, and to gain feedback about how well or poorly those requirements are being met. In the truly aligned organization, that learning finds its way into process improvements. This notion of the "customer's customer" is a powerful factor for building loyalty and alignment. In an unpublished paper entitled "Dynamics of the Customer Age" Lloyd Baird and Darrell Griffen define this factor as essentially becoming a "cocreator":

> To move beyond being simply a supplier to become integrated into and responsive to the organization, you have to move to becoming a cocreator of the goods and services. Your knowledge of the customer's customer will allow you to help [your immediate customer] to adapt more quickly and produce more efficiently. Because of your own network of relationships you can provide solutions that the customer simply cannot provide. [That customer] will depend on you to provide the input, help design the products and services and then redesign its own development and production system to respond

(Continued)

> to [the final customer's] needs. The role of co-creator is complex, but the value added to your customer is so great that you are more likely to develop a very long term relationship. As importantly, you will learn from the process and develop relationships that you can use as you work with your other customers.

The Zara Way

It is difficult to think of an industry in which knowing what customers want is more challenging than it is in the field of fashion—women's fashion in particular. What's in style today is out of style in a heartbeat, leaving clothing manufacturers and retailers in a cross fire of missed sales and hard-to-liquidate inventory. Spanish-based Zara has demonstrated an uncanny ability to keep pace with customer preferences and respond to them rapidly. Described as a "very quick fashion follower,"[2] Zara's product development teams stay close to the gyrations of customer preferences by attending fashion fairs, hanging out on university campuses, and going to the clubs patronized by target customers. Their aim is to catch each new fashion wave as it's forming. Zara's retail store personnel do their share by contributing timely sales data and trend analysis.

What Zara's people learn in the field and in company stores is rapidly communicated to product designers and production employees, who operate with very short lead times. Competitors design their clothing a season in advance on the basis of expected customer tastes and then contract for offshore production. Zara dances to a different drummer. With its pulse on today's tastes, it designs and produces for what people want at the moment. Its "sense and respond" system can design, make, and deliver entirely new fashion items to its stores worldwide in four to five weeks and redesigned items in just two weeks—an amazing feat. Most of its competitors need nine months to do that. Zara's system satisfies the desires du jour of customers and contributes immensely to the coffers of its parent company, Inditex.[3]

Delivering the Goods or Services

Operational processes that serve customers effectively and efficiently are another benefit of horizontal alignment. Understanding what people want isn't enough. You have to develop excellence at delivering what customers want where, when, and how they want it. How one develops that excellence is not a deep, dark secret. Whether we're manufacturing electronic equipment, handling loan applications, or running a restaurant, the quality movement has taught us how to make and deliver things and services faster, better, and at lower cost—and with continual improvement over time. Great things happen when people work together to find new and better ways of serving their customers—when they do the right things right.

A truly aligned company bases its processes on its strategy and on the information and learning that flow from customers and the marketplace. Process improvement in these companies is not an end in itself but a tireless servant of strategy and customers. To illustrate, let's return to Zara.

Zara's strategy is to know its customers so well that it can give them the fashion designs they want when they want them. This strategy greatly reduces the company's need to stock large inventories and helps it avoid the immense problem plaguing other clothiers: having to unload overstock and items that "didn't catch on." Zara's supply chain—its horizontal axis—is specifically designed to serve that strategy and is driven by customer information. As one writer described it:

> [Its] "fast fashion" system depends on a constant exchange of information throughout every part of Zara's supply chain—from customers to store managers, from store managers to market specialists and designers, from designers to production staff, from buyers to subcontractors, from warehouse managers to distributors.[4]

The company's organization, production processes, performance metrics, and physical spaces are designed with rapid and direct information transfer in mind. Further, whereas most competitors have shifted production to Asia to save money, Zara maintains a significant portion of its own production and even builds in some slack capacity. These things add to unit production costs but give Zara the dexterity its fast fashion strategy requires.

Employees Have Information and Are Engaged

A company can have all the information in the world about its customers and its customer-serving processes, but that will not do much good—and the enterprise will not be horizontally aligned—if information is tucked away somewhere where employees cannot see it or use it in a timely way. Great performers identify the critical success factors that underpin the Main Thing of the business and communicate them to employees at every level.

The leadership of one start-up dot-com company we recently encountered relies heavily on its CSFs to keep its people focused on the right things. Different employee teams have different CSFs. The team that works on developing the web portal, for example, receives updates on page feed time, the number of people who return to the site each month, and "click-throughs" (the number of visitors who go to the website's advertisers' links). CSFs are compiled daily and displayed on a computerized dashboard that management monitors and reports to all employees at its weekly all-hands meeting.

Sharing CSFs keeps employees focused and engaged on the parts of the business that truly matter. CSFs are an excellent tool for aligning employees with customers. But like every alignment tool described in this book, they work best when supported by meaningful incentives and other features of performance management.

Capabilities Meet or Exceed Customer Requirements

One cause of horizontal misalignment is a mismatch between a company's capabilities and the requirements of its customers. Many years ago, while working with Procter & Gamble on quality issues, we developed a simple 2 × 2 graph to help people understand this issue and its impact on company-customer alignment. The horizontal axis of that graph represented customer requirements, from low to high, and the vertical axis represented P&G's ability to meets those requirements, again from low to high. Alignment is complete when customer requirements and the company's ability to deliver are perfectly matched, as in Figure 4.2. This ideal situation is seldom achieved. In some cases, a company's capabilities lag behind customer requirements, creating disappointment. In others, company capabilities exceed customer requirements, creating the risk that the company will offer things that customers are not ready for.

Even when alignment is achieved, it has a natural tendency to fall apart. A company will either get ahead of its customers or fall behind. The resulting misalignment will take one of two forms: the catch-up gap or the opportunity gap.

The Catch-Up Gap

Whenever company capabilities lag customer requirements, we observe a catch-up gap (Figure 4.3). In the figure, customer requirements have advanced but the company's capabilities have not. It's

FIGURE 4.2

PERFECT ALIGNMENT OF CAPABILITIES AND CUSTOMER
REQUIREMENTS

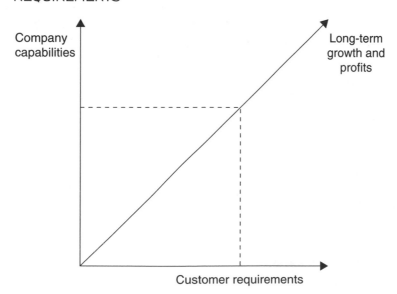

FIGURE 4.3
THE CATCH-UP GAP

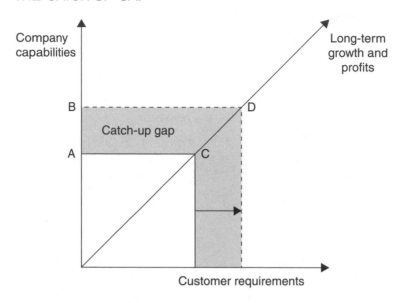

stuck at capability level A. The area between A and B on the vertical axis represents the catch-up gap that must be closed to meet customer requirements and capture increment C–D of growth and profits. This gap requires employees to go to heroic and often expensive lengths to satisfy customers.

Here are some examples of capability lags and the efforts that companies must undertake to close the resulting catch-up gap. Some are quality issues, but others are not:

Capability Lags	Catch-Up Penalty
Products fail to perform to expectations	Returns
Product breakdown or failure before expectations	Product replacements; warranty costs
Mistakes in order fulfillment	Reshipments; overnight shipping cost
Inferiority to competitor products/services	Lower price to get the business

| Inability to build and ship quickly enough to suit customers | Build costly inventories in advance of orders |
| Competitors outpacing you in providing value as perceived by customers | Constant racing to catch up; frustrated and exhausted employees |

Needless to say, growth and profitability suffer when capabilities lag customer requirements, as indicated by the 45-degree line in Figure 4.3. Even herculean rework efforts may fail to placate frustrated customers, and the cost of customer recovery will surely sap profits. According to one study, 91 percent of dissatisfied customers stop doing business with offending providers.[5] That's a high price to pay for falling short of customer expectations.

We often use the term *dead man walking* to describe companies mired helplessly in the catch-up gap. These are once-great enterprises that have rested on their laurels. Most are inwardly focused, oblivious to customers, competitors, and the market environment. To maintain profitability, they cut R&D, reduce headcount, and spend their time trying to find ways to produce the same old goods or services more cheaply.

Getting Out of the Catch-Up Gap

You're probably wondering: If my company is already in the catch-up gap, how can it get out and escape those catch-up penalties? Determining the cause or causes of the gap will lead you to the remedy. What got you into the catch-up gap in the first place? Did you lose touch with customer expectations? Have your products or services failed to keep abreast of technical advances? Does your company have a reputation for poor customer service? Are people frustrated trying to do business with you?

One approach to answering these questions is to have employees read customer comments and complaints. Another, more viscerally powerful way is to hear those complaints directly from the mouths of customers. For example, one of our clients, the president of a wireless company, invited defecting customers to attend a semiannual customer satisfaction "summit" with all expenses paid. As he saw it, the opinion of one defector was equal to that of 10 regular customers. All corporate executives and customer call center personnel were required to attend the summit. "The things they said were stunning," he told us. "The experience was uncomfortable and awful, but it was great medicine." In his opinion, the success of this summit was directly related to the degree to which customers made his employees squirm. The outcome was a dramatic reduction in customer defections.

Another technique is to benchmark the best practices of the market leaders and then institute the changes that will put you ahead of them on factors that matter to customers.

The Opportunity Gap

A very different situation prevails when a company's capabilities *exceed* customer requirements—when the company routinely satisfies current customer requirements and is able to address needs that customers haven't been able to imagine, much less articulate. This creates what we call an *opportunity gap*. The opportunity gap (Figure 4.4) is not about gold plating or adding bells and whistles of dubious value to already functional products or services. It's about perceiving the latent needs of customers and developing new products or services that delight them, as opposed to merely satisfying them—things that make them say, "Wow!"

In Figure 4.4, the company's capabilities exceed what it requires to satisfy current customer requirements. It has a capacity to surprise them, to raise their definition of satisfaction to a level they hadn't anticipated—to "wow" them. In so doing it can charge premium prices that will increase long-term growth and profitability. Competitors that cannot reach that level of satisfaction will fall behind.

It's difficult to think of a company that delivers more wow than Apple. Most personal computing customers are satisfied with their Windows PCs, but Apple's Mac users are not simply satisfied—they are remarkably devoted and enthusiastic. Whereas Windows machines have become commodity products sold largely on price, Apple's Macs

FIGURE 4.4
THE OPPORTUNITY GAP

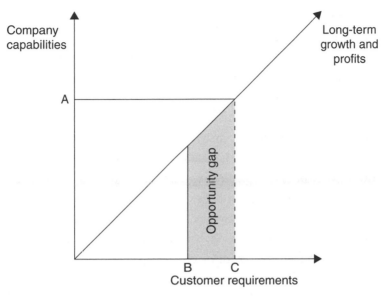

remain iconic, and people pay a premium to own them. The explosive success of the iPod, iTunes, the iPhone, and the iPad further demonstrates Apple's ability to outstrip customer requirement and exploit the opportunity gap for growth and profitability. Wisely, its new products are not so far out and unfamiliar as to provoke fear or reluctance on the part of potential customers. At some level, those new products are compatible with what those customers already understand. Although Apple is ahead of its customers, it isn't out of touch, and this is one of the reasons Apple is the world's most powerful brand.

The availability of wow products and services from a company such as Apple eventually raises customer expectations and requirements for everyone in the industry. As that happens, customer requirements shift to the right on the horizontal axis of Figure 4.4 to align with the most competent company's capabilities. This shift puts competitors into horizontal misalignment, lagging customer requirements. They now face the dreaded rework gap and must either increase their customer-serving capabilities or pay a price in terms of growth and profit.

Exploiting the Opportunity Gap

Being ahead of customers can be a curse or a blessing, depending on how you handle it. On the downside, if your offer is too far ahead of customer needs, people will not value or pay for it. For example, they may not see a need for all the computing power you've packed into your latest device. They may give you points for being a pioneer, but you can't take those points to the bank.

One way to exploit the opportunity gap—the preferred approach—is to coax customer expectations up to your higher level of performance. This puts competitors at an immediate disadvantage. Raising customer expectations may be accomplished by demonstrations or infomercials that help people appreciate—and desire—your greater capabilities—that make them say, "Wow!" Increasing people's comfort levels with what you offer is another approach. This can be done by means of test marketing or sample giveaways or by equipping "trendsetting" individuals and product reviewers with your products.

SERVICE BEYOND EXPECTATIONS

One of your authors, George Labovitz, had a wow experience not long ago at his summer home on New Hamphire's Lake Winnipesaukee. It was Friday morning, July 4, the beginning of a three-day holiday weekend. The weather was exceptionally hot and humid that day, with barely a breath of air shaking the pine trees or making ripples on the lake, and the weather forecast called for more of the same for the next few days. As bad luck would have it, George's air-conditioning system picked that morning to fail, leaving his house filled with weekend guests baking in the heat.

Because it was a holiday, George had no expectation of getting his air conditioner fixed any time soon. He'd just have to live with a houseful of cranky visitors for the next few days. But to get the repair process moving, he phoned Strogen's Service Experts in Rochester, the local heating/air-conditioning company that had installed the system four years earlier. "I didn't expect anybody to answer on the Fourth of July," he recalls. But to his surprise, a human being rather than an answering machine took his call. "We're closed for the holiday weekend," she explained, "but if you have a repair issue, I can have someone get back to you."

"That will be fine," George replied, giving the woman his address and phone number. Hanging up, he resigned himself to a long wait.

Three hours later and from 30 miles away, a burly guy named Jason, in a uniform and wearing a Boston Red Sox cap, was at his door. "Problem with yah ah conditionah?" he asked in a thick New England accent.

"I was amazed that this guy would be coming on such short notice," George recalls, "and on a holiday."

The repairman went straight to work, but after more than an hour of hard labor in the afternoon heat, he had bad news. "I found the problem," he reported. "Trouble is, I need to find the replacement parts to fix it. Be back at 9 a.m. tomorrow."

Find replacement parts on a holiday weekend? George wondered. What was the chance of that?

Surprisingly, the repairman and an assistant were back the next day at nine o'clock sharp, parts in hand. And within an hour, George and his guests felt the delight of cool, dry air wafting through the lakeside dwelling. Wow! You can bet that George would be a loyal Strogen's client for years to come and would recommend the company to his neighbors.

We told co-owner Mike Strogen about this experience and asked him whether his affiliation with a national service firm such as Service Experts contributed to his company's ability to deliver the wow to George. "We've always had a commitment to outstanding customer service," he said. "There's no other way to run a successful service company like ours, especially in a small

(Continued)

town environment. So when we were considering a relationship with Service Experts, it was important to us that they shared our commitment to customers. With them, we now have the means to provide a live person, not an answering machine, to answer the phone and directly contact our on-call service tech. It makes a big difference." He felt it was the shared values that permitted this big company–small town dynamic to provide excellent service to customers.

When Companies Can't Get It Right

We see many examples of companies that can't seem to get it right with their customers. Some drive into the future with their eyes fixed on the rearview mirror. Victims of their past success, these companies have lost touch with the expectations and requirements of today's customers. We call this the *phantom limb syndrome*, named after the medical phenomenon that makes people who have lost a limb feel that it is still there. Though customer requirements and needs have changed, these companies think and act as if nothing has changed.

Does your organization suffer from this syndrome?

In other misaligned organizations, process improvement is aimed in the right direction but fails to hit the mark because different employees and functions have different time and goal orientations. As we sometimes say, they "spin at different speeds." R&D people, for example, generally have a multiyear orientation whereas their colleagues in finance are on a quarterly regime and salespeople live from month to month. Time and goal differences can jinx attempts at cross-functional integration.

George Labovitz encountered a clear example of this problem at a large European maker of blue jeans. Key functionaries in that company had very different senses of pace. Its production manager, for example, would have been most happy if he had long lead times and could grind out hundreds of thousands of blue jeans in the same size and color. In his ideal world, all men would wear jeans with 34-inch waists and 33-inch inseams. Why? In his world of manufacturing, any alternation in the work process meant retooling, reordering, and retraining. The sales vice president's perfect world, in contrast, would be one in which the company produced all sizes in all colors and kept everything in stock. Why? Because in his world of sales, 13-year-olds change their fashion minds every Thursday. Metaphorically, the production guy was turning at 10 rpm and the sales guy was spinning at 100. The only thing they could agree on was that the people at corporate headquarters in Brussels were spinning at zero rpm.

You've surely encountered similar situations where you work. It's quite normal, and it's important that different people and functions spin at different speeds. Differentiation of skills and functions—so-called silos—is important. Would you hire a sales manager who was happy selling one-size-fits-all jeans? Of course not. Management's job is not to eliminate silos but to integrate differences and align them with the needs of customers. You do that by getting everyone oriented to the Main Thing and tuned to the voice of customers. This is accomplished by using every opportunity to communicate the Main Thing to different employee groups and by finding ways for these people to hear the voices of the customers—by having them meet customers, read customer comments and e-mails, and so forth.

Getting Horizontal Alignment Right

Successful horizontal alignment is achieved when everything people do and all the processes and incentives they use to create value are informed by the expressed and latent needs of customers. To say that businesses should listen to their customers and act on what they learn would be to state the obvious. Doing it well, however, is seldom easy. Here are just a few of the reasons why:

- What customers want can change quickly. Not convinced? Try getting a solid fix on the fashion needs of teenage girls.

- Customers don't always understand the technical possibilities for product or service innovation. Thus, if you ask them to describe, say, their ideal automobile, they'll usually describe a vehicle that is only marginally different from the one they already own. Unlike automotive engineers, customers are generally unaware of emerging technologies that would result in a stunningly different and more desirable automobile.

- Few employees are in direct contact with customers. They don't feel a responsibility for understanding customers and their needs. "I'm in finance. I never even see our customers."

- Some customers oppose real change. In his work on innovation, Clayton Christensen has pointed out the dilemma faced by technology companies whose customers tell them to "just keep doing what you're already doing. We're very satisfied." These customers have large investments in hardware, software, and systems; they are interested in upgrades, not breakthroughs that would require them to scrap what they have and make major capital outlays. Companies that listen to these customers tie their fortunes to technologies that will eventually end up on the scrap heap, which is why some people refer to this as the tyranny of served markets. In the end, those "satisfied" customers abandon their suppliers when a new and better technology becomes cost-effective.

Hearing the voice of current and potential customers isn't always easy. Nevertheless you must develop multichannel methods for gathering market data and disseminating the data throughout the organization. Among the best ways of doing this is by opening a clear channel between your organization and its critics. As Robert Burns wisely said, "O wad some Power the giftie gie us, to see oursels as ithers see us." Critical feedback from outsiders keeps us in touch with reality. Years of conducting alignment assessments has taught us that people generally think more highly of their performance than do their subordinates, peers, bosses, and customers. Perhaps it's human nature.

Having our shortcomings pointed out by others isn't pleasant. It can make us uncomfortable, even angry. Yet we need a dose of it now and then. Critical feedback from customers can be the most valuable information we can get. Consider the example of Rohm and Haas, a subsidiary of Dow Chemical. Several years ago, we were working with this company to improve its customer-serving processes. Seeking a reality check of its performance, the company set up a meeting with a key customer. Rohm and Haas wanted feedback from this customer on what it was doing well and not so well. That meeting was an eye-opener. Customer representatives brought along a matrix that rated Rohm and Haas and its other suppliers in key areas of performance and quality: materials, timely delivery, after-sales service, the knowledge of salespeople, price, and so forth. The matrix assigned a numerical grade for each supplier in each performance/quality category. Our client was measured as weaker than its competitors in several areas. Genuinely surprised, they asked the visitors, "Why didn't you tell us this? We would have corrected those problems." You may have already guessed the response: "You never asked."

Once you truly understand customers' needs, what it takes to delight them, and what they think of you as a supplier, you'll be prepared for the next step: aligning all your business processes, personnel programs, and performance measurement systems with them. Begin with the customers:

- Identify your key customers.
- Determine what would delight them.
- Create the capability and mechanisms to continuously gather actionable customer data and the ability to use it.
- Design a system to regularly measure the extent to which your customers are delighted.

Once you have the customer part of the horizontal axis under control, move on to the people and processes that serve them:

- Identify all core customer-serving processes.
- Reengineer processes to maximize performance.
- Set up a system for continuous process improvement and management.
- Design a system to measure and monitor process performance.

How One Organization Got Aligned

Camp Pendleton is home to the 1st Marine Expeditionary Force and numerous other operating units. It is the largest Marine Corps base in the western United States, occupying 125,000 acres along 17 miles of the California coastline north of San Diego. Locals joke that Pendleton is the only thing that keeps sprawling Los Angeles from gobbling up San Diego.

Naval Hospital Camp Pendleton (NHCP), a 72-bed facility with a staff of 2,100, has the job of serving the health needs of the base's thousands of warriors, their families, and area military retirees: roughly 150,000 eligible beneficiaries. When we became acquainted with it, this relatively small hospital was carrying a heavy burden: it annually dealt with 561,000 outpatient visits, 5,000 inpatient admissions, 1,600 births, and 4,100 surgeries. Like many civilian and military health systems, however, NHCP hadn't always been at the top of its game in the areas patients cared most about: access and timeliness of care. That situation was seen as an opportunity to improve by Navy Captain Mitch Heroman, a neonatologist who had been appointed the hospital's commanding officer. He and his team committed themselves to a turnaround effort that within three years achieved amazing results. NHCP was recognized for excellence in many areas. Its maternal infant service captured the Malcolm Baldrige California Excellence Award. Dr. Heroman was the recipient of the American Hospital Association's Federal Healthcare Executive Award for Excellence. Other recognition followed.

What accounted for this turnaround?

George Labovitz had traveled to Camp Pendleton to discuss the alignment and tracking tool that Heroman's regional admiral had commissioned for NHCP and for the huge Naval Medical Center San Diego ("Balboa") down the coast from Camp Pendleton. While in San Diego, George learned of the turnaround and drove up to Pendleton to take a look.

When George arrived at Heroman's office, he spotted a copy of our first alignment book on the desk. The many Post-it notes sticking out from its pages indicated that he'd read it with care. That book had sold tens of thousands of copies, but as authors we could never know how many people actual read it, much less followed our advice. Dr. Heroman had done both. As he explained, he and his staff had used the "Five Big Questions" cited in the book as the starting point of their effort to improve hospital performance through alignment with the needs of its customers.[6]

1. What do our customers care about the most?
2. How satisfied are customers with us in terms of the things they truly care about?
3. How can we move beyond satisfying to delighting them?
4. What are the best-of-the-best companies doing to delight their customers?
5. In what ways, if any, do customers find it difficult to do business with us?

His tool for answering most of these questions was a sample survey of actual patients. By chance, the administrator of a major civilian medical center, a reserve naval officer, had been assigned to the hospital's staff to fulfill his active duty requirement. Heroman put that officer to work interviewing patients he encountered in the hospital's many waiting rooms, 90 patients in all. Patients were asked a series of open-ended questions designed to determine their top three needs and how they ranked those needs. The survey determined that patients wanted the following, in this order:

1. Competent and caring physicians who would spend time with them
2. Rapid access to appointments
3. Courteous staff members who respected them

Following the concepts in our book and taking "We care for marines and sailors who are first to protect us and our way of life" as their Main Thing, the NHCP team brainstormed the things they could do to exceed their customers' expectations—to delight them. For instance, they would attempt to provide same-day appointments for primary care and much shorter lead times for specialty appointments. Staff members were encouraged to go beyond courteous service: they were empowered to say yes to patient requests (only their supervisors could say no) and to deliver quality healthcare with compassion. A central appointment center was established; access to it was measured and feedback was given to the clinics. In fact, all the improvements undertaken by the team were measured, and regular feedback was given to the staff. Dr. Heroman believed that "if it cannot be measured, find something else to fix."

To gain insights into how best to deliver customer delight, team members looked to other customer service organizations. Their research led them to USAA, a financial services company that had delighted active duty and retired military officers for more than 80 years. The subject of many business case studies and articles, USAA had earned a reputation for unbeatable integrity and service to military people and their families. It was one of the rare enterprises that totally understood its customers and their needs and responded effectively. More than 90 percent of military officers had accounts with USAA. In fact, almost everyone on the NHCP team was a USAA customer.

Among its other strengths, USAA had a reputation for quickly answering incoming customer calls and handling requests; those were critical elements in the NHCP team's definition of patient access. It was judged the best-of-the-best company to benchmark on this aspect of customer delight. A similar system was installed at NHCP.

Turning improvement ideas into real working processes required many staff meetings, planning, the development of performance metrics, process mapping, and a practical use of information technology. Captain Heroman (now retired) notes:

> In addition to technical improvements, clear goals, and measures, we also celebrated our mission—our Main Thing. Whenever any employee—whether a housekeeper,

someone from supply, a physician—was seen delivering compassion to patients or doing anything that was above and beyond, we celebrated at the next scheduled command gathering called a "Captain's Call." We'd tell their story and present them with a beautiful coin that had the hospital's logo on one side and the Marine Corps and Navy flags and our values—Honor Courage Commitment—and "One Team One Fight" on the other side. These coins became known as "Compassion and Getting to Yes Coins." I'm very happy to say that I gave out many of these to our wonderful NHCP Health Care Team members.

All that work paid off. In less than three years, measurement confirmed huge progress:

- Less than 1 percent of patients failed to obtain same-day appointments.
- Less than 4 percent of incoming calls to the central appointment center were abandoned (meeting the USAA benchmark, the best in the industry).
- Appointments with specialists were scheduled in nine days or less.
- People who had opted for off-base civilian providers in the past returned in droves as NHCP's reputation changed. Ninety-four percent of eligible patients enrolled in NHCP, at the time the highest percentage in the Department of Defense hospital system.
- NHCP scored one of the highest scores ever on ODI's alignment and tracking tool.
- The hospital had the best retention rate of active duty personnel in the U.S. Pacific Fleet and Marine Forces Pacific.
- NHCP was rated number one among 30 Navy healthcare facilities.

The icing on the cake was the U.S Navy Surgeon General's Customer Service Award to Naval Hospital Camp Pendleton.

Reflecting back on what powered NHCP's success, Heroman cited the principles of alignment, in particular its focus on the Main Thing:

> If I had to choose the one thing that made the biggest difference, it would be rallying everyone around our Main Thing: caring for marines and sailors who are first to protect us and our way of life. That mission drove everything. We began every policy and resource meeting with the question, "Will our decision be good for the marine and sailor?" And we ended every meeting with "Was the decision we just made best for the marine and sailor?"

That's the story on horizontal alignment. We'll pick it up again in Chapter 5, where you'll learn how to make the processes that deliver value along this axis better and better.

Key Points on Horizontal Alignment

- Horizontal alignment integrates systems and processes with the needs of customers.
- People in horizontally aligned entities understand what customers want and how they prefer to be served.
- Horizontally aligned work processes can be changed rapidly as customer requirements change.
- Suppliers who learn to exceed customer expectations create an opportunity gap that can produce competitive advantage and premium pricing.

Things to Do

Ask your internal or external customers to answer these questions:

1. What do you need from me?
2. What do you do with my output?
3. Are there gaps between what you need and what you get?

FIVE

Better and Better: Continuous Process Improvement

↑
Process defined
Improvement-building principles

The focus in Chapter 4 was on achieving horizontal alignment, beginning with customers: learning about them, figuring out what they want, and pushing beyond satisfaction to delight. Customer delight results from exceeding expectations for price, design aesthetics, quality, usability, consistency, or whatever it is that people value. More than satisfaction, delight immunizes customers from the temptation to look elsewhere; it generates loyalty, repeat business, referrals, and competitive advantage.

What we didn't spend much time on in that chapter, however, are the processes that create and sustain customer delight. How can we design our processes to be better aligned with customer needs and to produce goods or services faster, better, cheaper, or whatever else makes customers say "Wow"? This chapter answers that question. Outstanding processes—processes that get better and better as we learn more about our customers and our capabilities—are an essential ingredient in horizontal alignment.

But first a definition: A *process* is a set of repeatable activities or steps that transforms inputs, such as material and labor, into outputs:

goods and services. Every business, for example, has a process for ful-
filling customer orders. A fulfillment process may be good, bad, or
downright ugly. A good one may take just a few minutes to complete
and involve a few competent employees, ending with consistently
accurate fulfillment, shipping, and billing. An order process that's
downright ugly, in contrast, may require days to complete and involve
many more people, culminating in fulfillment, shipping, and billing of
inconsistent quality. These are the companies that mail you the wrong
shoes in the wrong size with the wrong billing amount.

Today's top-performing companies don't make these mistakes.
They have outstanding processes, and they stay on top—and stay
aligned—through continuous process improvement. Their people
examine and reexamine key processes in an effort to find and eliminate steps and/or activities that fail to add value for customers. For
them, making processes better and better is almost a religion.

ORIGINS

Continuous process improvement is a feature of the quality
movement that emerged from the minds of several American
thinkers in the 1930s, took root in postwar Japan, and began
spreading throughout the developed economies in the 1970s.
Japanese industry, however, deserves credit for developing and
perfecting continuous process improvement, which they call
kaizen. Kaizen was Japanese industry's response to the problem of scarcity in the difficult years after World War II. Because
capital, materials, and skilled labor were all in very short supply, the country's industrial leaders were desperate to eliminate
waste and make the most of what they had. Continuous process
improvement was one of their solutions.

Different approaches to improving quality and operational performance
have been implemented over the years: Total Quality Management,
Reengineering, Six Sigma, and the current favorite, Lean Management.
You may have been involved with one of these approaches. In cases in
which these programs have not lived up to expectations, the cause often

has been a failure to understand that continuous improvement is as much a mindset as it is a technique: a way of looking at the workplace world. The idea that the journey toward process excellence is never over must become part of the culture. If it doesn't, management will pocket its short-term gains, declare victory, and move on.

It has been our privilege to work with dozens of companies that attempted to implement one or more of these methodologies. Many were successful in the short term. Those which have produced gains over the long haul share some behaviors, which we call the pillars of continuous quality improvement. These companies

Do the right things right

Think big, aiming for major leaps in efficiency and performance

Map every process step

Always ask "Why?"

Never allow too many cooks in the kitchen

Think and act systematically

Eliminate fear

Build a culture of continuous improvement

Measure and remeasure process performance

In the rest of this chapter we'll examine those behaviors in detail.

Do the Right Things Right

Process improvement and our concept of alignment are solidly united when people do the right things right. Doing the right things is about being aligned with customer needs and being effective in delighting customers. To know you're doing the right things, ask two questions:

1. Is there a customer who cares about what we're doing? For example, it's been estimated that 25 percent of work can be stopped and no one will notice or care because customers have moved on.
2. Do you know what the customer's requirements are? If you don't know what customers care about, how can you know what to do?

Doing things right is about executing well—about being efficient. Doing the right things right, being both effective and efficient, is an unbeatable combination.

We've had lots of fun over the years with this concept. We show clients a 2 × 2 grid (Figure 5.1) with the concept's four possibilities. The lower-left quadrant indicates the absolutely worst space to be: doing the wrong things wrong. This is where you're shooting yourself in the foot with every move; you're neither effective nor efficient. The upper-right quadrant is the ideal place to be: doing the right things right. Here, what you do is aligned with what customers need and value, and you're very efficient at doing it. The other two quadrants represent the other two possibilities: doing the wrong things right and doing the right things wrong. Neither one will win you laurels.

FIGURE 5.1

THE RIGHT THINGS RIGHT GRID

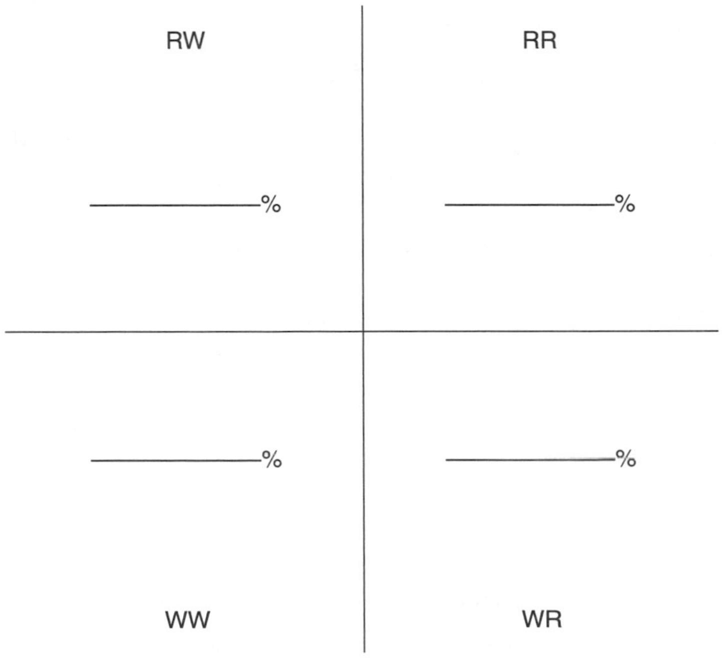

Even the best companies fall into the wrong/right trap now and then. We witnessed a vivid confirmation of this some years ago when we introduced our grid to FedEx's senior managers. CEO Fred Smith sprang from his seat, came up to our flipchart, and pointed to the wrong things right quadrant. Turning to the group, he exclaimed: "This is our problem! Our pilots fly the airplanes perfectly. Our mechanics fix the airplanes perfectly. The trouble is we're flying the wrong damn airplanes—and I'm the guy who picked them." That was many years ago. The company has since transitioned to a fleet of aircraft with higher fuel economy, lower emissions, and greater flexibility.

When we show the grid to clients, we ask them to estimate the percentage of their time that falls into the grid's quadrants. These should sum to 100 percent.

For many years we kept track of the percentage of the time our client participants reported spending (or wasting) in each quadrant of the 2 × 2 grid. Here's the average of their self-reported numbers:

Wrong things wrong: 8%

Right things wrong: 17%

Wrong things right: 24%

Right things right: 51%

The fact that managers report doing the right thing right only about half the time is a bit shocking. And that's the average; some do much more poorly. One major consumer goods firm we worked with had a right things right score of only 40 percent. When we flashed that number on the screen, the president stood up and turned to his managers. "Do you know what that means?" he asked. "It means that the company would be better off if we all stayed home two days a week!" After much laughter, someone in the back of the room shouted, "But which two days?"

What percentage of the time are you and your colleague doing the right thing right? Process improvement will not take you very far if the leadership is directing employees to do the wrong things with greater and greater efficiency.

Think Big

Newcomers to process improvement are unaccustomed to the idea of big, big improvements. For them, an improvement of 10 to 15 percent would be just fine. One client of ours, a multinational apparel maker, suffered from limited expectations. Its product design process stretched out over 60 weeks, and that was for very basic and uncomplicated apparel items. It required 60 weeks to do what competitors were accomplishing in 10 weeks.

When we first met this company's managers, they told us that their goal was to cut time out of the process. "Well, how much time are you aiming to cut?" we asked.

"We want to get it down to 45," they said. To us, 45 days seemed an aggressive but feasible goal in light of the simplicity of the company's products.

"No," they said, "we're not talking about days. Our goal is to design and launch new products in 45 *weeks* instead of the current 60."

This company was not thinking big enough. It needed to enlarge its expectations. Even if it reached its improvement goal of 45 weeks, its ability to design and launch new products would lag far, far behind the capabilities of its competitors.

Contrast the apparel company's modest goals with that of a New York City bank that was more ambitious in its process aspirations. This bank's process for approving loans over $5 million took six weeks to complete. Those six weeks included abundant time that did nothing to improve the quality of the bank's loan decisions. Documents sat on people's desks for days at a time. Incomplete or error-ridden files had to be sent back for rework. Meetings were interminable and generally inefficient. Meanwhile, the bank's more agile competitors were stealing its customers.

Responding to the chairman's request to examine the problem, we mapped the entire loan approval process, which was found to contain 32 steps involving personnel in five departments. Instead of flowing smoothly through those many hands, loan application files would pass from one department to another, then back to the first department for more work. Each handoff added time but little value.

Our analysis fingered the chairman as a major time waster in the loan approval process. Because his signature was required by the bank's policy for large loans, decisions were sometimes delayed for a week or more while he was traveling. Other bottlenecks caused work to pile up, adding still more time to the process.

Shocked by our report, the bank chairman asked us to fix the process. With his approval, a process improvement team set a goal of reducing the number of steps from 32 to 8 and the number of individuals who directly touched the process from 41 to 9. Those were challenging goals, but the team attacked them with vigor. Some steps were combined; those that added no real value were eliminated. Technology was applied wherever it was useful and cost-effective. Sources of frequent error were "goof-proofed." Finally, the chairman's role was limited to unusual cases in which his judgment was absolutely necessary. In the end, the process was reduced from six weeks to four days with no perceptible reduction in the quality of loan decisions. Because many fewer people were involved, accountability for process performance was much clearer.

Take a look at the processes with which you're involved. Count the number of steps. Then consider how you could slash that number. Above all, think big!

Map Every Step

To improve a customer-serving process, begin with a detailed understanding of the existing process. That is accomplished through process mapping. A process map defines in flowchart form the exact path through which inputs are turned into goods and/or services. It specifies the entire end-to-end sequence of steps and activities, the exact numbers and types of inputs, and who has responsibility for each activity. Finally, the process map defines quantitatively what constitutes successful output. For example, in the bank loan example described above, the improved process map stipulated that the approval process for loans $5 million and higher had to be completed within five days.

In process mapping, all activities or steps are laid out from the customer back into the organization. Alternatively, activities may be mapped from the point at which the process is initiated (e.g., a field salesperson submits a customer order) to the point at which the process is complete (e.g., the customer's order is filled and billed). Regardless of which approach is taken, each step is analyzed to determine whether it is adding value to the final output. Steps that fail to add value are eliminated, redesigned, or combined as needed. In conducting process analysis, we always ask the following questions:

- Which activities add more cost than value?
- Where are the opportunities to do things faster and better?
- What steps can we eliminate without reducing value to customers?

Because time is usually of value to the company and its customers, we ask people to look for tasks that can be done in parallel rather than in linear fashion. For example, auto manufacturers reduce vehicle assembly time by building components such as engines and transmissions in parallel with body assembly. Those components arrive at the assembly line as they are needed.

Always Ask "Why?"

When something is wrong with process output—or a single step— ask why and keep asking until you get to the source of the problem. Toyota understood this when it developed its concept of Five Whys, which has proved to be invaluable in tracking down the root cause of quality problems

Here's how it works. If you have a problem, ask "Why?" When you get an answer, ask "Why?" again. And again. By the fourth or fifth answer you will usually uncover a systems cause of the problem rather than human error. Root causes are usually hidden, so look beneath the symptoms of problems and what appear to be obvious causes.

Here's an example: Customers complain that service techs often have to return more than once to fix an appliance.

Q: Why must they return?

A: They don't have the right parts in their trucks.

Q: Why don't they have the right parts?

A: Dispatchers aren't collecting specific and relevant information about the appliance.

Q: Why aren't they collecting the necessary information?

A: Inadequate technical training of dispatchers.

Suboptimal output from a business process always has a root cause. Your job is to find and eliminate it by redesigning the process, eliminating a step, providing better training, or some other means.

Never Allow Too Many Cooks in the Kitchen

In theory, everyone who is involved with or touched by a business process should be involved in its improvement. In practice, however, it's best to limit the number of participants. Do you remember the expression "Too many cooks in the kitchen will spoil the broth"? Too many cooks involved in a process improvement effort will slow the effort, diffuse accountability, and make project management issues more difficult. We observed this problem at one of our client companies, which had 30 people on a single process team. Some had nothing useful to contribute, and more than a few were outright barriers to progress. Because so many of these people traveled on business, finding meeting dates that would accommodate their schedules was extremely difficult. Weeks would sometimes slip by without progress. By the time we came on the scene the team leader had nearly lost her mind.

Our client and friend retired Vice Admiral Wally Massenburg, the commander of the Naval Air Systems Command (NAVAIR), encountered this problem in his effort to resolve a particular aircraft engine problem. Over 200 people—Navy people and civilian contractors—showed up for his first meeting. No one wanted to be left out or considered uninterested in the admiral's big project. Few of those people, in Massenburg's view, had anything to contribute, and so he set up a simple rule then and there: team participation would be limited to people who, in his words, had the ability to make decisions and contribute "stuff"—his shorthand for knowledge, experience, funds, or other resources. Before that initial meeting ended, the admiral had sent all but 15 people back to their jobs. Fifteen of the "right" people would get a lot done; 200-plus would be a mob and spend most of their time stumbling all over one another.

When you form a process improvement team, limit participation to individuals who can make themselves available and who have something positive to contribute (stuff). Each person should have experience and expertise in one or more of the areas touched by the process, and all of them should have skin in the game: accountability for the change they will create.

Think and Act Systematically

Because alignment is concerned with the entire system, management must shift its focus from optimizing the work of individual departments or particular processes to optimizing the horizontal flow of outputs across the entire organization. That system view helps us integrate different functional areas of expertise that would, if left to themselves, turn into isolated and self-interested silos. Indeed, we want to give people in different departments and functions a larger perspective—a view that is broad enough to see all the tasks being performed, how those tasks serve the Main Thing and customers, and how their own work fits in. This is one of the challenges faced by every organization that attempts process improvement. It is also a fundamental feature of horizontal alignment. Here are some tips for integrating a systems view with continuous process improvement:

- Start with end customers and work back from them into the organization.
- Identify all the steps that make up the process.

- Identify the steps that create value for customers and eliminate or redesign those that do not.

- Ensure that your steps create a smooth and uninterrupted flow toward customers.

Once people see the big picture, they can usually figure out how to improve their part of the total activity flow and how best to work with other units. They are also more likely to feel engaged with the organization and its strategy, feel valued, and commit to doing their best work. Once they have that broader vision, they will step out of their silos and work with others in making business processes fewer, faster, less costly, and more effective. The leader's job is to help managers and employees groups see themselves as partners in a larger team in service of larger goals.

Systems thinking should be buttressed with systems-oriented action and support. All systems in the organization—planning, budgeting, scheduling, performance management, and so forth—need to support the continuous improvement effort. Here are some examples:

- Improvements should be recognized and rewarded.
- IT systems should be designed to provide necessary information in a timely way.
- Training in process improvement tools and techniques should be universal and offered regularly.
- The hiring process should identify individuals for whom the concept of continuous improvement is a deeply embedded personal value.
- Senior management should be visible and unstinting in its backing for improvement efforts.

Eliminate Fear

One impediment to process improvement is people's fear that a reduction in process steps and a streamlining of activities will put them out of work. That fear is justifiable and, if not addressed, will create active resistance to whatever you are trying to achieve. People's fear must be replaced by trust that a pink slip will not be their reward for doing the right thing: eliminating waste and inefficiency. Yes, process improvement often reduces the number of hands needed, but smart organizations handle that issue through normal attrition or by moving affected employees to other—and, one hopes, better—jobs within the company.

People must also be unafraid to admit to their mistakes. Continuous process improvement is all about asking questions, exposing problems, admitting mistakes, and learning. People need to know that it is safe to point out problems and try different ways of working. They need to see problems as opportunities for improvement. Our colleague Y. S. Chang, former chairman of the quantitative methods department at Boston University's School of Management and a recognized authority on quality and process improvement, used to refer to problems as treasures because each one provided an opportunity to make things better for customers.

Remarkable things happen when fear is driven from the workplace and people feel safe in exposing problems. Consider the case of a hospital that was trying to improve its practices. One of the areas being looked at was medication error, a fairly widespread source of injury and even death in the U.S. hospital system. The "official" error rate for wrong medications at this particular hospital, however, was very low—lower than anyone in the business would reasonably expect. What was going on? When investigators asked how this could be, the nurses revealed an ugly truth: many medication errors were simply not reported out of fear of retribution. Once management committed itself to a policy of not punishing people for pointing out mistakes, the error rate briefly rose as people told the truth, then came down as the same people openly discussed the problem and found ways to eliminate the causes of medication errors.

Build a Culture of Continuous Improvement

Organizational culture is the collection of attitudes, values, norms, assumptions, and beliefs that guide people's behavior. An improvement-oriented culture gives no ground to "good enough." The issue of process quality is not considered permanently settled; instead, an attitude that "there'll always a better way" is baked into the workplace. That attitude animates people to pursue that better way. You don't see that attitude in organizations that lack an improvement-minded culture. There, people know about problems but no one wants to deal with them. It's much easier to sweep them under the rug.

TIPS FOR BUILDING AN IMPROVEMENT-MINDED CULTURE

During our work with Motorola, a senior executive told us how they built a culture of continuous improvement. We summarize his remarks as follow:

1. Begin with measurement.
2. Make continuous improvement a strategic imperative.
3. Tie continuous improvement to the performance management system.
4. Train, train, train.
5. Hold senior management reviews
6. Have goals for everyone

Leaders have the greatest responsibility for creating and maintaining a culture of continuous improvement. To quote the first of Dr. W. Edward Deming's 14 points of management, leaders must "create constancy of purpose towards improvement."[1] They cannot, as often happens in failed attempts to institute quality methods, launch a training program, give a few pep talks, and go back to obsessing on the next quarter's results. Instead, leaders must provide the constancy of purpose that Deming advocated. They do that when they

- Keep the organization laser-focused on customers
- Support and reward improvement-oriented behavior
- Involve everyone in the improvement agenda
- Provide training and resources
- Listen to employees and empower them to act

Equally important, the leadership team must maintain sustained commitment to continuous improvement in both words and deeds. Consider this example. When the Iraq war began, we were facilitating a meeting at the headquarters of the Air Mobility Command. The room was full of generals. A one-star general said to the commander, a four-star general, "A war has started. Is this meeting on quality mandatory?" The four-star replied, "No, but I'm staying." So they all stayed and did some very good work, launching a model quality improvement program that eventually received a presidential award.

FedEx, which embodies the concepts of alignment and quality, has demonstrated sustained commitment to continuous improvement through its enterprisewide program of Quality Driven Management. Its leaders never lighten up in their support for QDM. As Fred Smith told his 300,000 employees in a recent Message from the Chairman:

> A proven way to boost profits is through *continued, relentless pursuit of quality improvement* [our italics], which has always been a key premise at FedEx. Quality Driven Management (QDM) has helped FedEx team members work smarter and deliver improved customer experiences over many years.
> It's at the heart of our ability to deliver on the Purple Promise: "I will make every FedEx experience outstanding."

TO INCREASE EFFICIENCY, REDUCE PROCESS STEPS

Confirmation of the benefits of reducing the number of process steps was provided to us by an engineer who likened the handoffs between linear process steps to the resistance encountered at each connection point in an electrical circuit. As he explained, if you have six handoffs, multiply each handoff by the efficiency between steps. For example, if a process is so well designed that each handoff provides 95 percent efficiency (or .95), we lose only 5 percent at each handoff. Five percent doesn't seem like much, but when we multiply $.95 \times .95 \times .95 \times .95 \times .95 \times .95$, we discover that the efficiency of the entire circuit is only 77 percent.

The more handoffs in the process, the lower the total efficiency. Thus, reducing the number of non-value-adding steps is a simple yet effective way to improve process outcomes. Improving the efficiency of each step has a similar positive impact.

Measure and Remeasure Process Performance

Organizations that succeed with process improvement measure and remeasure, and what they measure is determined by what matters to customers (e.g., fast on-time delivery, product reliability, accurate order fulfillment) and to the company (e.g., throughput time, product returns, cost). These enterprises take the temperature of how well their processes are performing both internally and externally. They establish baselines and chart progress against them. More important, they act quickly when measurement indicates a problem.

Take a minute and think about your organization or your piece of it, whether it's a division, a department, or a work team. What does it measure and how often? What does it do with those data?

We hope that this chapter has gotten you thinking about the processes you use to serve customers and how you can improve them over time—not by a little but by a lot! Continuous process improvement is the most powerful weapon in your arsenal for horizontal alignment. It is also a huge source of competitive advantage. A company that can quickly reconfigure or improve its processes in response to its environment has a bright future. Consider the case of Apple's Chinese supplier of the iPhone's glass screen.

Weeks before the first version of the now ubiquitous iPhone was scheduled to be shipped, Apple engineers made a design change. They would use a glass screen instead of a plastic one. That single alteration produced ripples through the company's Asian supply chain, including a line overhaul at an assembly plant in China. But because assembly plant personnel were agile and responsive, they met Apple's critical and demanding schedule. As described in the *New York Times*, 8,000 workers were awakened in the dead of night, given a cup of tea and a biscuit, and transported to the assembly plant as the glass screens arrived from another supplier. Within an hour, they were churning out iPhones by the thousand. "The speed and flexibility [of that plant] is breathtaking," one executive told the *Times*. "There's no American plant that can match that."[2]

Chances are that you can't rouse your employees from their beds in the middle of night. Still, are your operations fast, flexible, always improving, and ready for whatever comes down the pike? If you answered yes to those questions, you have the makings of a horizontally aligned organization and a promising future.

During the years we've been advocating alignment and teaching its methods, we've seen enough before-and-after situations to appreciate the power of continuous process improvement in all types of organizations: manufacturers, service providers, shipping companies, government bodies, and healthcare institutions, to name just a few. We've seen how clients have learned to align and rapidly realign strategy, people, and processes with the needs of their customers. And many have achieved impressive results. Again, the sign that they had truly become aligned was that they were simultaneously able to see improved results in customer satisfaction, employee metrics and profitability all at the same time!

A freight rail company, for example, improved its safety performance dramatically, rising from seventh to first in its industry. Its billing accuracy went from 87 percent to almost 98 percent, and the reliability of its locomotive fleet doubled.

A wireless communication enterprise reported a 116 percent increase in its new customer accounts, even as customer defections dropped by 11 percent. Its cost of acquiring each new customer account decreased by 23 percent, creating a $35 million savings. Customer and employee satisfaction indicators increased in all markets and at corporate headquarters. Customer CHURN was reduced 11 percent, equaling a $35,000,000 gain That wireless firm was named among Fortune's top 25 EVA companies.

Improvements like those are neither unusual nor limited by industry when the job of alignment is done right. A trucking company we worked with increased its billing accuracy by 50 percent, advanced from number 3 to number 1 in customer satisfaction, and became its industry's profit leader and set safety records in 5 out of 6 key measures. A joint company-customer team cut loading/unloading costs by 50 percent.

Operational improvements like these should be reward enough. However, there's another benefit: the practice of alignment will make you a more effective manager. More aware of what's going on. More in control.

Chapter 6 describes a relatively new tool for enhancing alignment on both the horizontal and vertical axes: social media.

Key Points on Continuous Process Improvement

- A process is a set of repeatable activities or steps that transforms inputs, such as material and labor, into outputs— goods and services.
- The masters of continuous process improvement practice all or several of the following improvement-building principles:

  Do the right things right.

  Think big, aiming for major leaps in efficiency and performance.

  Map every process step.

  Always ask "Why?"

  Never allow too many cooks in the kitchen.

  Think and act systematically.

  Eliminate fear.

  Maintain systematic support for the improvement effort.

  Build a culture of continuous improvement.

  Measure and remeasure process performance.

Things to Do

- Estimate the percentages of your work team's time and activities that fall into the quadrants of the grid shown in Figure 5.1. They should sum to 100 percent.

We do the wrong things wrong.	_____ %
We do the right things wrong.	_____ %
We do the wrong things right.	_____ %
We do the right things right.	_____ %

- Think about our list of improvement-building principles. How does your organization rate against each of the following principles using a scale of from 1 to 5 (with 1 being the lowest rating, 5 being the highest):

  We think big when making process improvements. _____

  We map every process step. _____

  We always ask "Why?" when we find a problem. _____

  We never allow too many cooks in the kitchen when working on process improvements. _____

  We think systematically. _____

  We have eliminated fear. _____

  Our leaders maintain systematic support for continuous process improvement. _____

  We have a culture of process improvement. _____

  We measure and remeasure process performance. _____

SIX

Social Media as an Alignment Tool

How Walmart uses social media for internal alignment

Capturing the voice and ideas of customers at Starbucks and LEGO

"Democratized" innovation

Creating buzz for the Ford Fiesta

When we wrote our first book on alignment, the term *social media* had barely entered the lexicon. Since then it has become a part of contemporary life, both personal and professional. Some people are hooked on it. From our perspective, social media has given us a powerful new approach to rapidly realigning an organization's strategy, processes, people, and customers in the face of constant changes. We see its emergence as a paradigm shift in communications.

Historically, management relied on one-way, hierarchically directed communication. It controlled information, sending down messages such as a change in strategy without inviting or encouraging feedback. Communication with customers was also limited. Companies told customers what they wanted them to hear. Customers had few opportunities to respond except with their purchase decisions.

As participative management became popular as a way of increasing employee motivation and commitment, a two-way communication process developed in which information flowed down, up, and across the organization, with employees providing input on decisions that affected their work. The extent of employee participation, however, was still controlled by management.

Social media platforms have dramatically reshaped communications. They have opened organizations to voices that cannot be tightly controlled by management—both inside and outside voices. For management, there is a downside and an upside to all this. On the downside, management gets an earful of things it may not want to hear, including things to which it may not know how to respond. On the upside, this communication revolution has taken some problems off management's back. Management no longer has to have all the answers, especially at granular levels of detail; employees can take on more of the burden of figuring out how work should be done.

In this chapter we dig into the new and exciting subject of social media and learn how several pioneering companies are using it to enhance alignment both internally and with their customers.

Social media is a spectrum of Internet-based technologies that includes short- and long-form written text (e.g., Twitter and blogs), online chat rooms, online personal and professional networks (e.g., Facebook and LinkedIn), and video sites such as YouTube. Unlike traditional broadcast media, social media is fueled by user-generated content; this has transferred a substantial segment of communications from the hands of government, the mainstream media, corporations, and other officialdoms to the control of individuals.

In less than 10 years, this new form of communications has altered the way people interact with friends and business associates, the way companies connect with their employees, and the way employees connect with one another. Consumers can now talk to one another about the merits and demerits of products and services in a way that only they can control. Whatever they plan to purchase—an automobile, a pair of winter boots, or catering services—it is now possible to tap the direct experience of consumers who have already taken the plunge. "I was disappointed with my new boots," as one customer of a famous retailer commented on its website. "The water-resistant lining did not work as advertised. I had to send them back." Consumer ratings like that one, pro and con, are all over the Internet today, and corporate marketing people have no way of controlling them.

Social media have also given companies, their customers, and their employees new opportunities to communicate and engage with one another for mutual benefit on a number of levels. This makes social media a powerful tool for rapidly achieving both vertical and horizontal alignment. This chapter explains how that works.

Social Media for Vertical Alignment

As was described in Chapter 2, vertical alignment connects and engages employees with the organization's strategy. As we emphasized there, leaders cannot achieve that connection and engagement by simply making a stand-up presentation or sending everyone an e-mail. That type of communication rarely sticks. To make an impression and change behavior, a new strategy must be repeatedly described and explained. Questions must be answered. People need to understand how their participation will make the strategy work and how their participation will be valued. To accomplish this, leaders must engage with employees on the things they can do—daily routines and unit initiatives—to make the strategy work. That engagement will not happen unless employees trust management and the messaging process. People must believe that management's goals and strategies will benefit them in tangible ways, such as opportunities for personal advancement, greater job security, higher pay, and bonuses. Vertical alignment is strongest when people are convinced that a strategy is good for them and is something they can trust. The new social media technology can provide the platform for employees to get onboard with the strategy.

As was noted earlier in this book, much has happened over the last 10 or more years to erode employees' trust in their leaders and organizations. They've seen coworkers furloughed and pay levels frozen. They've watched as production and customer service jobs have been shifted to low-wage countries. They've observed as mergers and acquisitions strategies have eliminated entire departments and related personnel and many of those strategies have failed to deliver. Yes, leaders must engender trust if they want people to get connected with their agendas.

The Internet technology that enables today's social media has made trust building more challenging and at the same time more possible. Management once controlled most of the information worth having—about salaries, customers and customer feedback, product reliability, and competitors. Today, anyone with an Internet connection can obtain much of that information, putting himself or herself in a better position to evaluate messages from the C-suite. That same technology empowers employees to discuss among themselves—and with outsiders—the merits of what they hear from management. If used thoughtfully, however, social media can be a tool for generating trust and bringing people together in service of the Main Thing as well as management's strategy for achieving it. That tool can make it easier for employees to communicate with management and with one another about strategy, comment and ask questions, and get answers. Many companies are leading the way by experimenting with social media programs.

Small organizations are less challenged in connecting with employees on strategy and building trust because the physical and social distance between leaders or owners and employees is much reduced. These people see and speak with one another many times during the day, and they pick up important nonverbal information cues that their counterparts in big organizations cannot. They have many opportunities to engage in dialogue about what the company is trying to accomplish and what each person is doing to make it happen. Even when participants have very different views, dialogue increases the likelihood that they'll eventually be on the same page.

How can you accomplish this if you're Walmart, a huge company with over 2 million employees in 8,900 locations? A company CEO might send out a communiqué or video. He or she might speak to employees through a webinar, a form of social media (though it is a one-way talking head format). Top-down, unidirectional communication forms of this sort, however, don't engage people at the visceral level, which is what alignment requires. Most of what people hear is quickly forgotten. What's needed is two-way communication and not just between employees and management. True buy-in takes place when employees can check in with one another, ask questions, and exchange ideas and opinions.

Is your organization using social media to connect directly with people about the Main Thing of the business? Does it communicate regularly about its strategy? Before its merger with Oracle in 2010, the CEO of Sun Microsystems put out a weekly blog in which he discussed his company's strategy and progress, and he invited feedback (aka engagement). Does anything prevent your CEO from doing the same thing? Do employees have opportunities to dialogue with their managers and peers about strategy, changes, and things they can do to make the strategy successful?

If you're coming up with lots of "no" answers, your organization should identify social media formats that can help it generate dialogue and engagement on strategy.

Social Media for Horizontal Alignment

The social media platform capabilities we've described can also be used to achieve horizontal alignment, first by integrating the disconnected and inward-looking silos and second by opening clear channels between customers and the employees who serve them. Let's consider the potential and application of each.

Internal Connections

The size and complexity of today's organizations has necessarily produced specialization of functions: production, HR, finance, marketing, legal, and so forth. The expertise developed within these functions is a very necessary response to the complexity in the modern world of business. That expertise has real value, but there's a downside. As you've undoubtedly noticed, functional areas of expertise tend to become self-interested, self-protecting silos that fixate myopically on their unique concerns at the expense of the broader view. Although this is natural, it challenges leaders to find ways to capture and integrate the energy and know-how of different functions in the service of strategy, customers, and the Main Thing of the business.

Understanding this challenge, Walmart has developed a password-protected MyWalmart.com site that its U.S. employees can go to 24/7, from home or from work, to obtain information, share ideas, and communicate with fellow employees. The site's format and content are based on what employees want and the way they want it. One part of the site allows individuals to check work schedules and benefits, learn about merchandise discounts, and find job openings within the company. Another part allows them to connect with other Walmart personnel. Encouraging employees to talk to one another about the issues facing their local stores is a powerful way to engage them, get them working together on problems, and achieve alignment. It also gives employees opportunities to state their views and offer suggestions, a modern version of the traditional suggestion box. The site's content management system makes it easy for approved users to create and post their own content.[1]

MyWalmart.com has been wildly popular with employees. Within 18 months of its launch, 920,000 employees registered on the site, and close to 85 percent of users return to it weekly.

RULES OF THE ROAD

The ability to voice one's thoughts and post blogs through company-owned social media is a new freedom. Like all freedoms, however, this one should be tempered with some basic rules, such as the following:

- **Take personal responsibility for whatever content you post.**
- **Identify yourself as the content's author.**
- **If what you say differs from your organization's official position, indicate that you are expressing a personal viewpoint.**

- Respect copyrighted materials. Post only with permission from the copyright holder.
- Disclose your sources.
- Do not post confidential information.
- Never quote another person without that person's permission.
- Make no personal insults or attacks.

Internal sites such as MyWalmart.com have some of the same purposes as traditional employee surveys: finding out what's on people's minds and how they feel about the workplace. At least one qualitative difference, however, is worth noting: a survey is a snapshot—a picture of the workplace at a specific moment in time. It may take weeks or months to pull all responses together and summarize their meaning, by which time things may have changed. An employee site, in contrast, is not a picture at a particular point in time. It is dynamic, constantly changing and staying current with feelings and issues. That timeliness has huge advantages for decision makers. It provides a real-time thumb on the pulse of the employee population.

Knowing What We Know

Large, multilocational enterprises have always had a hard time collecting, storing, and reusing the knowledge and experience of their many bright employees. Every employee knows something that could help one or more of his or her colleagues if a simple and effective knowledge-sharing mechanism were available. Consider this hypothetical example. Bill, an engineer in Philadelphia, has run into a complex production issue. He'll spend days studying the problem. Bill doesn't realize that Sarah, who works in his company's Chicago plant, encountered and solved the very same problem the previous month. Consider the value that Bill and Sarah's company would reap if Bill knew what his Chicago colleague has already learned.

Bill's situation exemplifies the knowledge management problem that big consulting, engineering, and other technical companies have been struggling to solve for decades. The advent of social media has brought solutions much closer. PricewaterhouseCoopers, the giant tax consulting–advisory firm, for example, has developed a social media site called iPlace to solve the "knowing what we know" problem.[2] It is used to tap into the collective knowledge of over 30,000 people. In its first year of operations, iPlace generated over 2,000 ideas, 10,000 comments, and 40,000 votes. Among the factors that made this approach work, according to the company, were the following:

1. *Leadership involvement.* On the day the site went live, PWC's U.S. chairman challenged employees to share ideas that would improve the business. Other firm leaders participated as well. This demonstrated management's support for the idea-sharing initiative.

2. *Simplicity.* The iPlace site was designed to be user-friendly and easy to navigate. Visitors could do only one of three things: offer an idea, make a comment, or cast a vote.

3. *Anonymity.* The identity of site participants was limited to names, not job titles or levels of authority. This put the focus on the value of the ideas offered, not on the status or authority of the individuals offering them.

4. *Fast response.* Senior people made a commitment to respond to every idea within 30 days.

5. *Transparency.* Employees were told how their ideas had been assessed and why they would be adopted or rejected.

External Connections

There has always been a boundary between the internal world of the enterprise and the external world of suppliers and customers, with a narrow communication pipeline between them. Marketing has traditionally controlled most of that pipeline's bandwidth. Its advertisements send information to customers. Salespeople, customer service personnel, and market researchers act as receivers of the customer's voice, filtering and then transmitting what they hear to decision makers in the enterprise. The volume and quality of communications that pass through this pipeline is often mixed.

Social media provide opportunities to break through the boundary that separates enterprises from those they exist to serve; they bring customers inside, where they can speak directly and without a filter to decision makers and employees. And social media do it *fast*—in the moment. There is no need to spend a month designing a customer survey, another month to implement it, and yet another month to figure out what it all means (by which time reality may have changed). Technology-based social media generate and regenerate real-time information, but simply collecting data is not useful unless there is clear accountability about who is collecting it, analyzing it, and acting on it. One of the commitments a company implicitly makes when it encourages customers and employees to share ideas is that the company will respond to contributors in a meaningful way. That response may require the company to take action when there is an issue that can compromise quality for the customer or expectations for the employees.

Generating Ideas Through My Starbucks

Starbucks provides a good example of a customer-directed application of social media. In early 2008 the company set up a "My Starbucks" page on its website (go to Menu -> Learn More -> My Starbucks Idea to see it)[3]. By using this site, customers can make suggestions and comment on the suggestions of others. Within the first three years, site visitors offered over 100,000 ideas about coffee and tea drinks, food products, music and merchandise, the application of new technology, the in-store customer experience, environmental responsibility, and several other categories. These suggestions are visible to all site visitors, who can "vote" and comment on them. By the end of the third year 130 customer ideas had been adopted and launched within the Starbucks system. For example, one person recommended that stores shorten customer waiting times by having two separate service lines: a fast one for brewed coffees and a second one for drinks that require extra preparation, such as espressos, cappuccinos, and lattes. When

30,000 customers expressed support for the idea, Starbucks worked out a plan and began pilots of the two-line system in several of its Chicago-area locations.

My Starbucks' user suggestion operation is highly transparent. Site visitors can see which ideas have been launched, which are under development, and which are being considered. This application of social media is proving to be a powerful but low-cost approach to bringing the customer voice inside. It appears to have many advantages over most traditional forms of market research, including customer focus groups.

Kids' Stuff at LEGO

LEGO did something very similar. Finding itself in desperate competition with video and other electronic games, the company began soliciting ideas from kids for exciting new ways to use LEGO products. A page on its site (http://city.us.lego.com/en-US/Gallery/Challenges/Default.aspx) introduces a video clip in which staff designers challenge kids to create and submit ideas for cool new uses for LEGOs. In the video, designers show kids the different formats in which their ideas can be submitted. To date, this challenge concept has provided LEGO with thousands of ideas. Each year 100 of the best ideas are selected, and their creators are flown to the company's design studio, where they work directly with the design staff to flesh out their creations. Prototypes of those new creations are sent gratis to dozens of LEGO fans with an invitation to try them out, provide feedback, and discuss them on the site with other users. This approach has engaged many people and expanded interest in LEGO products.

Eric von Hippel has coined the term *democratized innovation* to describe this new approach to product and service development that (1) encourages customers to articulate precisely what they want and (2) provides a convenient channel for them to communicate their needs and ideas and comment on product or service initiatives proposed by companies.[4]

Creating Buzz for the Fiesta

Marketers are also finding ways to use social marketing to raise awareness of current or soon-to-be-launched products and services. These forms of communication may have a greater influence over people than do traditional ad campaigns. People are so inundated with ads that they've learned to block them out. For most of us, communications received through noncompany sources—independent bloggers, tweeters, friends and acquaintances, and so forth—are much more credible. Ford Motor Company's successful use of social media in the launch of its new Fiesta model in North America provides insights into the potential of this approach to customer communication.

Ford launched its European-designed Fiesta vehicle in North America in 2011, but before it did, it prepared the beachhead with a clever program of social media promotion. Ford's website announced a contest that would give 100 people free use of a new Fiesta for six months. The only obligation for the winners was that they develop content on a theme one might describe as "me, my Fiesta, and my life." The winning 100 applicants, however, were not chosen at random. Ford marketers selected "connectors" and "influencers": bloggers, trendsetters, and individuals who had a large presence in the world of tweeting (some had tens of thousands of followers). These people were soon writing about life with their new Fiestas. One described using her Fiesta to deliver Meals on Wheels to shut-ins. Another reported using the car for an elopement. During the six-month period, the 100 winners distributed thousands of written and filmed pieces through social media. Those pieces generated enormous buzz in the auto-buying marketplace (one YouTube video racked up 4.3 million hits), which contributed to the Fiesta's successful takeoff. By Ford's accounting, the program generated 50,000 leads to interested buyers and 35,000 test drives, feats that would have cost millions to duplicate through traditional promotional techniques. And 10,000 Fiestas were reputedly sold in the first six days after the official launch—a very good start for a new car model.

APPROACH SOCIAL MEDIA STRATEGICALLY

Like any other important function, social media should be approached strategically, with the right people involved and with goals that align with the larger aims of the organization. For a thoughtful discussion of this subject, see H. James Wilson, P. J. Guinan, Salvatore Parise, and Bruce D. Weinberg, "What's Your Social Media Strategy?" in the July–August 2011 issue of *Harvard Business Review* (www.hbr.org).

Whether they are customers telling vendors what they want, vendors trying to discover what will delight customers, or executives attempting to rally people around a new strategy, all benefit from an environment in which people can connect with one another. Social media such as the ones we've described in this chapter make that type of environment possible.

Key Points on Using Social Media for Alignment

- Effective use of social media requires clear strategies and process owners.
- Different platforms, such as internal websites, external websites, Facebook, and Twitter, have different audiences and require different strategies.
- You cannot be half committed if you go down the social media road; this communication avenue must be supported and managed.
- Company social media platforms require guidelines and policies.
- Senior management's participation is critical to social media effectiveness.
- Social media is a culture changer.
- In using social media, different strategies are required for vertical and horizontal realignment.
- Sponsors of social media must be clear on their goals and provide adequate resources.

Things to Do

- To enhance vertical alignment:

  Sketch out a social media strategy for reaching different groups in your organization.

  Indicate how social media can be used to stimulate employee-management dialogue.

  Design a structure for sharing comments, questions, and responses.

- To enhance horizontal alignment through social media:
  Identify three ways to bring in the voices of customers.
  Explain how social media can tap into your top two market segments.
  Indicate how an internal website could be used to provide employees with customer comments and complaints.

SEVEN

Culture: The Secret Sauce

Why culture matters

A workable definition

How changed behavior can alter attitudes, beliefs, and values

Using a culture dig to uncover a company's culture

The leader as culture architect in chief

Culture is always with us, like the air we breathe, yet we are seldom conscious of it and many people can't put a finger on it. If asked to describe the culture of our country or our organizations, we struggle to find the right words, yet we know that culture exists and that it matters.

For some companies, culture is a source of strength and competitive advantage. It's their secret sauce. Google, Procter & Gamble, and Apple, for instance, have cultures that foster the consumer-centricity and innovativeness that keep them healthy. Walmart's culture encourages people to think of change as their friend—a good thing, not something to be feared. At Walmart the thinking is, "If we are not changing today, we are in trouble." What would happen at your workplace if people thought that way? Zappos, the successful online footwear apparel vendor, has a culture in which change is welcomed. Its website tells job seekers, "If you are not prepared to deal with constant change, then you probably are not a good fit for the company." That speaks volumes about Zappos' culture. The company recognizes that competitors can copy its online commerce site, its shipping methods, and so forth, but as its website states "as long as embracing constant change is part of our culture, they will not be able to evolve as fast as we can."[1] That statement echoes something that Victor Rosansky learned directly while working with the late Sam Walton, founder of Walmart. After a two-day workshop, Victor jokingly asked Walton, "Sam, would you mind if I were to share everything I've learned about Walmart with your competitors—it would guarantee my children's college funding?" Walton laughed and said, "Go ahead. I know my competitors' cultures, and they could never do what we do." In the years that followed, we worked with some of those competitors and learned that Sam Walton was right!

The importance of culture was noted by Lou Gerstner as he reflected on his experience in transforming the then listless IBM. "I came to see, in my time at IBM," he wrote, "that culture isn't just one aspect of the game—it is the game."[2] James Heskett documented the impact of culture on operating performance in *The Culture Cycle,* in which he identified four sources of competitive advantage gained through an effective business culture. He calls them the Four Rs: the *retention* of good people who care about the business and contribute to its success; *referrals* from current employees, which lowers hiring costs; *returns* to labor that yield higher productivity per compensation dollar; and *relationships* with customers that improve customer loyalty. His research suggests that the Four Rs can explain up to 50 percent of the difference in operating performance among companies.[3]

Yes, culture matters, and the right culture—the appropriate culture for a company's strategy—can make organizational alignment much easier. This chapter will show you how. But first a definition. Culture is the product of four dynamically related components: attitudes, beliefs, values, and behavior (Figure 7.1). Among these components,

FIGURE 7. I

THE DYNAMIC RELATIONSHIP AMONG CULTURE'S KEY
COMPONENTS

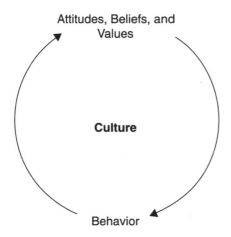

attitudes, beliefs, and values are difficult to change because they are
deeply ingrained, particularly values.

Trying to directly change attitudes, beliefs, and values is incred-
ibly difficult if we attack them directly. The faster, surer way is to
approach them indirectly through the one component of culture over
which management has some control: people's behavior. It is easier
to get people to behave their way into a new way of thinking than to
get them to think their way into a new way of behaving. Thus, when
management changes behavior and then demonstrates how the new
behavior results in better performance, better pay, greater job security, or opportunities for advancement—things that people value—
something remarkable happens: beliefs, attitudes, and values change.
Remarkable but true. Thus, what we call culture can be changed indirectly by changing behavior.

Cognitive dissonance is the mechanism by which changes in
behavior can change beliefs and attitudes. Leon Festinger, the social
psychologist who coined the term, found that an uncomfortable psychological tension is aroused when people behave in ways that are
inconsistent with their beliefs. That tension leads people to adjust

their beliefs to fit their behavior rather than the other way around. For example, most of us believe that lying is wrong, yet there are times when we are less than totally truthful. The inconsistency between our belief and our behavior creates psychological discomfort. To get rid of that discomfort, we alter our belief about truthfulness a bit. "A little white lie never killed anyone," we tell ourselves. Our behavior has made a change in our belief.

The same thing happens in the workplace. As an example, consider the case of the staff at a nursing home. The general attitude among the low-paid frontline caregivers was that the patients were unappreciative, uncooperative, annoying, and too quick to complain. That attitude permeated the employee culture.

A new nursing home director was quick to notice and wanted to change the culture to one that was more patient-centric and empathetic. She didn't hire a hypnotist to alter her staff's beliefs and attitudes toward patients; instead, she focused on changing their behavior. "Starting tomorrow," she told them, "I want you to visit each of your patients, greet them with a 'good morning,' and spend two to three minutes talking with them about whatever interests or concerns them at the moment."

The staff people were dubious but followed the boss's instructions. They gave their morning greetings and talked with patients not just about their problems but about their children and grandchildren. A funny thing happened. After a week of the new morning regime, the staff began to see the patients with new eyes—not as unresponsive, complaining old people but as individuals who had real lives that staff members could make better through their work. In other words, their attitudes toward patients changed, and the culture of the nursing home changed for the better. Behavior led to a change in beliefs and attitude.

Culture and Alignment

The right culture greases the skids, making rapid realignment possible. People will readily embrace a new strategy or support an improvement initiative if it is consistent with their attitudes and beliefs. For example, if the culture is defined by a spirit of management-employee collaboration, and if that culture values service to customers, creating horizontal alignment across different functions will be relatively fast and easy. The reverse is also true. If a culture is dominated by fear and risk avoidance, a new strategy based on the introduction of innovative new products is not likely to be embraced by the rank and file. Consider pre-bankruptcy General Motors. That company had a bureaucratic, risk-avoiding culture in which new ideas were analyzed to death and had to survive the gauntlet of an approvals committee. Needless to say, innovations were few and slow in finding their way to auto showrooms. When management asked for more innovation, the culture resisted. It took a near-death experience to make management and employees realize that the old GM culture had to go.

Now that we have seen how important having the right culture can be in rapidly deploying and executing strategy, let's take a look at your culture. We'll start by asking a few questions: What is your organization's culture? What are its dominant attitudes and beliefs? What do people value? Is the culture supporting or impeding the alignment of behaviors and the organizational mindset you need to be successful? The following section offers a tool for answering those questions.

Conduct a Culture Dig

You can learn a lot about an organization's culture by simply asking: What does a person have to do to get ahead here? How would people at your company respond to that question? Perhaps they'd say that to get ahead you have to do one or all of the following:

"Be a practical innovator. This company lives on a steady stream of new products."

"Make your boss look good."

"Excel in sales. Around here the path to the corner office runs through sales."

"Do your job and keep your head down."

"Think outside the box. Be a maverick."

What does each of those statements says about organizational culture? Which would apply to your company?

That quick and direct question—What does it take to get ahead?—can tell you a lot about an organization, but it cannot capture the many nuances of culture that shape it. For that, we need a more powerful tool: the *culture dig*. This tool was suggested to us by a cultural anthropologist who had learned to study societies in her fieldwork through a similar framework of inquiry. The culture dig looks at four attributes or indicators of organizational culture:

1. Artifacts and symbols
2. The stories people tell
3. Relationships such as networks
4. The rituals and rules that guide behavior

Whether you are looking at a start-up company with 10 people or a multinational corporation, these four attributes help define the organization's culture. Table 7.1 shows the four attributes of culture and lists their typical manifestations. They are the things we generally look for in a culture dig.

Now let's explain more of what we mean by the four culture attributes investigated through a culture dig.

Artifacts and Symbols

Culture reveals itself through physical artifacts and symbols. We can learn a great deal about a company, for example, by simply observing the physical layout, beginning with the parking lot. In a hierarchical culture, some people have preferred parking spaces. You might ask, "Were those preferred spaces assigned to people who had done something extraordinary, or were they simply given to bosses?" Traveling from the parking lot into the building, you might ask, "Who has a private office, and who doesn't?" In most places, office size depends on the occupant's place in the pecking order.

TABLE 7.1
ATTRIBUTES OF CULTURE

Artifacts and Symbols	Stories	Relationships	Rituals and Rules
• Logos	• Heroes/heroines	• Reporting relationships	• Dress code
• Physical arrangements of space/furniture	• Successes/failures	• Networks	• Public acts of recognition
• Titles	• Hirings/firings	• Communities of shared interest	• HR policies
• Parking assignments	• Super salespeople	• With whom people speak, eat, engage in recreation	• Standard operating procedures
• Language	• Inventors	• Physical proximity to others	• Formal gatherings
• Information transfer	• Leaders	• Informal coalitions	• Rites of passage
• Planning timetables	• Crisis stories	• Spheres of influence	• Daily routines
		• Subcultures (e.g., techies)	• How decisions are made
			• Performance metrics

Where people sit during meetings also has symbolic meaning. We may observe, for example, an unspoken seating arrangement, with *numero uno* taking a commanding position. His or her lieutenants are seated to the immediate left or right, and the foot soldiers sit farther away. What do these arrangements tell you about organizational culture?

Even the office nameplates used by organizations have symbolic cultural meaning. Fancy metal name or title plates screwed into office doors signal hierarchy and a certain permanence or rigidity. This and related symbols must go if you want to have a more nimble, nonhierarchical culture with greater employee participation. Companies with that type of culture use symbols to signal what they stand for. Wall space at some Procter & Gamble locations, for example, is used to display performance charts. Those charts say in effect, "We measure and respond to the things that matter." Another of our client companies has a prominent "Wall of Fame" where photographs of outstanding employees from all levels are displayed.

Sam Walton, the founder of Walmart, was a man who understood the power of symbolic acts. In one well-publicized episode, he paid a surprise visit to a store. While walking about, he found a large stockpile of inventory in a back room. This was a serious departure from the company's inventory management doctrine, which was a key source of its competitive advantage. Without a word, Walton found a large sheet of plywood, a hammer, and some nails and used them to seal the door. He then informed the store management that no one was to use the inventory. It was to be picked up by the next delivery truck and redistributed within the system. The symbolism of his act was unambiguous: just-in-time inventory management was how business was to be done.

Symbols say a lot about the kinds of organizations we have—whether they are hierarchical or participatory, rigid or flexible, inventive or by-the-numbers. What artifacts and symbols would we find in your workplace, and what would they tell us about your organization's culture?

Stories

Stories are verbal artifacts that reveal values and beliefs. Countries have them, and so do organizations. Some stories are factual and feature heroes and heroines who personify the values the culture holds dear. Others stray into mythology. For independence-minded Scotsmen everywhere, the story of William Wallace (aka Braveheart) continues to be a source of pride and inspiration centuries after his death, and generations of American children still learn stories (much embellished) about Davy Crockett, the nation's iconic frontiersman and free spirit.

Corporate entities also recount tales of their own heroes. For years people at AT&T would tell and retell the story of the lineman employee who left his home and went out into a raging snowstorm on Christmas Eve to fix a downed phone line in his community. Employees at Minnesota-based 3M continue to remember and admire Dick Drew, an inventive lab technician who joined the company in 1924. Today's company lore recounts the persistence and dedication that led Drew to the development of masking tape. Drew had gotten the idea of developing a slightly sticky tape during a visit to an auto body shop, where he observed workers struggling with a two-tone paint job. He speculated that a low-adhesion tape that could be removed without surface damage or blemishes would make painting jobs easier. He began working on the idea when he returned to the lab. When company president William McKnight told Drew to stop wasting time on his idea, the inventor agreed but took his work underground, using whatever resources and personal time he could scrape together. Within two years he had a product that the company could manufacture and sell, and it became a cash cow for 3M for more than 70 years.

Drew's example has inspired generations of 3M employees and has had a profound effect on the company's culture. Rather than fire Drew for insubordination, McKnight learned from the episode and incorporated that lesson into his philosophy of management. From that point forward, 3M's management encouraged employees to exercise the kind of initiative McKnight saw in Drew. Today, the company's 15 Percent Rule allows researchers and developers to spend up to 15 percent of their time on their own projects.

Relationships

Relationships represent the formal and informal connections between people in an organization. They include reporting relationships, temporary alliances, and interpersonal interactions. Relationships are usually patterned along lines of authority, networks of communication, and spheres of influence. Authority-based relationships are usually obvious. Others are not as obvious but are often more important.

When doing a culture dig, we typically ask these types of questions in order to understand relationships: Who talks with whom? To whom do people look for approval or authorization? Who has lunch with the boss and who doesn't? Who is copied on memos? Whom do people consult when they need feedback?

Rituals and Rules

Rituals and rules include formal policies, practices, and ceremonies that are written or verbally sanctioned by the leadership. They also include informal acts that represent "the way we do things around here." For example, in highly bureaucratic cultures, issues are passed up the chain of command for resolution; decisions require many meetings involving many people. Admission to the executive dining room is a rite of passage for up-and-comers. Office dress is formal and codified. Parties are given for employees who have completed 25 years of service.

The culture of nonbureaucratic organizations is markedly different. Problems are resolved on the spot by the few people closest to the action. Dress can be casual, and the social boundaries between people with different organizational status are low.

Moving between organizations with markedly different rules and roles can be shocking. An associate of ours described the culture shock and frustration he experienced after moving from a fairly entrepreneurial firm to a job at a major university. "Everyone in our unit [at the university] had to be involved in every decision," he said, "even people who had nothing to do with the issue and had zero accountability for the outcome. Worse, everyone's opinion had equal weight, even people who had no experience or expertise in the matter at hand." By his own admission, our associate was the only person frustrated and shocked by this approach to decision making. "Everyone else had grown up in the university culture. For them, this was normal."

> **Tip:** Don't get hung up on fine details during a culture dig. Doing so will sap progress and bog down your team in debate. Instead, concentrate on the most important features of the culture—those with the most widespread and significant impact on people's attitudes and day-to-day activities.

Specify the Desired Culture

Once you've done a culture dig, you'll have a good sense of your culture's distinctive attributes. The big question is: How appropriate are the behaviors and attributes in light of the Main Thing of the business and its strategy? Clearly, a culture that's appropriate for one enterprise with a particular strategy may be inappropriate for one with a very different strategy. For example, for McDonald's, a by-the-book culture is much more appropriate than one that encourages and rewards independent thinking by its young, low-skilled, and often temporary employees. To be successful, a McDonald's restaurant must run like a finely tuned machine, delivering meals with speed and consistency. The corporation has spent years developing, testing, and refining the processes that make that possible. A franchisee would be crazy to toss out McDonald's proven operating manual and encourage employees to be creative. However, that culture would be totally inappropriate for a Wall Street bank, whose strategy depends on the inventiveness and 120 percent effort of its highly motivated personnel.

Cultural appropriateness truly matters. As Booz & Company wrote in one of its reports, "the particular strategy a company employs will succeed only if it is supported by the appropriate culture attributes."[4] But what are the appropriate cultural attributes for *your* strategy? To answer that question, put your current culture out of mind and begin with a clean slate. Ask, If we could start from scratch and design the most effective culture for our strategy, what would it look like? To answer that question, start by asking, "What behaviors will help us achieve our strategic goals?" Then, using the four attributes of culture listed at the top of Table 7.1 as a guide, work with your team to describe the cultural attributes that will foster the desired behaviors. What would its symbols and artifacts be? What stories would you like to hear told about the company, and what heroic deeds would they recount? What relationships would you see in this brave new workplace? What rituals and rules would channel people's behavior in the right direction?

If you and your people address those questions thoughtfully, you'll have a portrait of the culture that will foster the behaviors required to execute your strategy successfully.

Suppose, for example, that our strategic goals are more growth and greater innovation. What behaviors are needed to achieve these goals? In our practice we would approach this question with careful organizational analysis and a matrix like the one shown in Table 7.2. The left-most column of that matrix defines the behaviors we need to grow the business and stimulate more innovation: in this example, more risk taking, collaboration among employees, and rapid responsiveness to customers.

TABLE 7.2		
MATCHING BEHAVIORS WITH STRATEGIC GOALS		
	Strategic Goals	
Behaviors	**Growth**	**Innovation**
Risk taking		
Collaboration		
Rapid responsiveness to customers		

The next question is: What attributes of culture will foster those behaviors? To increase innovation, analysis might indicate that we need to inspire more risk-taking behavior; a culture that has driven out fear and that celebrates well-intentioned failures would be an example. To encourage collaboration, we may determine that the culture should reward team success. Likewise, increasing the speed of customer responsiveness might be facilitated by giving frontline employees the ability to act on the spot.

CHANGING BEHAVIOR AT PIXAR

As an example of how architecting the right behaviors can have an extraordinary impact, consider how Steve Jobs redesigned office space at Pixar to foster behaviors that would support collaboration and creativity. As President of Pixar in the late 1990s, Jobs understood that his people needed constant outside stimulation to think afresh. His problem was that the tighter his development teams became, the more insular their members' behaviors would become. He wanted to change that since he knew that creativity was a function of how many networks and external interactions his developers utilized. To promote network behavior and personal interactions, Jobs built a giant atrium in the middle of the Pixar building in which he put coffee bars, food stands, and eventually all the bathrooms. And it worked! The atrium became a place where people naturally congregated, and talked about their projects, and shared ideas. And over the last decade, Pixar has raised the bar of animation standards with each new movie, winning top awards and blowing revenues off the charts.[5]

To complete our method, we include metrics. Metrics tell us how well the new behaviors are working—that is, how well they are contributing to our strategic goals. They also reinforce continued progress, since people need to know that what they are doing is paying off!

In Table 7.3 we've extended the matrix to incorporate the cultural attributes and metrics just described.

TABLE 7.3
CULTURAL ATTRIBUTES AND METRICS THAT SUPPORT THE RIGHT BEHAVIORS

| Behaviors | Strategic Goals | | Cultural attributes | Metrics |
	Growth	Innovation		
Risk taking			Celebration of well-intentioned failures	New products per year
Collaboration			Team rewards	Number of team projects
Rapid responsiveness to customers			More employee discretion	Service time reductions

Identify the Culture Gap

If you have followed our advice so far, you now have pictures of two cultures: the one you have today and the one that is most appropriate for your company in light of its strategic goals. By comparing the two, you'll be able to identify what we call the *culture gap:* the areas where the current culture falls short of the culture you need. Your job as a cultural architect is to close that gap.

In some cases small, innocuous-seeming things can be impediments to closing the gap and fostering a more appropriate culture. We learned this lesson many years ago at a Ford Motor Company plant in Canada where management and unionized employees were so distrustful of one another that they could not collaborate in the resolution of serious production line problems that threatened the future of the plant. We decided that the best way to get at those production problems was to first break the culture of distrust and negativity that permeated the plant. With that in mind, we brought management and frontline workers together and asked the workers, "What bothers you when you come to work each day?" To our surprise, the most bothersome thing on the employees' list was the plant parking lot. With hundreds of cars arriving and departing with each shift change, workers often had to drive around for 10 or 20 minutes to find a parking space. Snowy winter weather and the placement of concrete traffic control barriers here and there compounded the problem. Seeing the assigned parking spaces for managers next to the main entrance added insult to injury.

This seemingly small issue—parking—had become a symbol of the them-versus-us rift that divided the plant and undermined productivity. "Okay," the plant manager said as he left the room, "I'll take care of it." A few moments later he had rejoined our meeting.

Within an hour we heard the sound of heavy equipment coming from the parking lot. A gigantic crane was busily moving the concrete barriers that restricted traffic in the lot. By the end of the day, the signs that marked off management's designated parking spaces were gone. Henceforth, parking was first come, first served. The union people were stunned. Small as the plant manager's single act of listening and responding may have seemed, it changed attitudes and, by extension, altered the culture of the plant.

Be a Culture Architect in Chief

Culture change is a big subject, and we've only scratched its surface in this chapter. The tools we've offered, however, can help you shape the culture of your workplace in ways that will align behaviors with strategic goals.

The top leader, of course, has the greatest responsibility for culture—and the greatest power to do something about it. As architect in chief, the leader should do the following:

1. Decide which behaviors are needed to pursue the strategy and meet customer needs.
2. Design the set of cultural attributes that will foster the right behaviors.
3. Ensure that attitudes, beliefs, and values are aligned with the Main Thing of the enterprise, with strategy, and with the needs of customers.

The culture architect should use every opportunity to mold the culture by telling the stories, articulating the core values, and implanting the right set of symbols and incentives. More important, leaders at every level have an obligation to prescribe the right behaviors. As we stated earlier, changing people's behavior is the easier way to change beliefs and attitudes. People must see consistency between organizational values and the behavior of their leaders. More important, leaders must model the behaviors they want others to follow. People must see consistency between the actions and stated values of their leaders.

Upholding the culture and maintaining consistency is particularly challenging for geographically expanding enterprises. How can the leader assure that the culture is consistent from one office to the next, from one continent to another? One firm that has found the answer is Abraaj Capital. Headquartered in Dubai, Abraaj Capital is a leading private equity manager that invests in emerging markets, including the rapidly growing economies of the Middle East, Africa, Turkey, and Asia. It is value-driven, investing only in companies whose operations are managed with values that are consistent with its own. The firm takes a responsible shareholder approach, looking at governance models, sustainability, impact on job creation, the environment, and human rights—values that are consistent with the UN Global Compact initiative.

Abraaj Capital's success depends on its ability to capture knowledge from a constant and abundant flow of information. As the CEO, Mustafa Abdel-Wadood, told us, success is about "sharing information, knowing what's relevant, being able to compile that information in some kind of meaningful way, and choosing what is worth acting on so that the right decisions can be made." Because 30 nationalities are represented in the company and employees are geographically dispersed, doing this is far from easy.

However, success for Abraaj Capital also depends on the ability to export its culture, which is based on the values of its founder, Arif Naqvi. That culture values a strong work ethic, diversity, entrepreneurism, collegiality, and empathy. It also emphasizes a long-term investment horizon and behaviors that develop trust and loyalty on the part of investors. Important behaviors include information sharing, understanding and serving customers, and avoiding the entanglements of internal politics.

As the firm grows, Mustafa has designed mechanisms for quickly aligning new people with the Abraaj culture. When a new office is opened, he assigns several Abraaj veterans to it. Those individuals act as carriers of the Abraaj DNA, its culture. New people are brought to headquarters in Dubai to learn how the business works and to develop formal and informal networks. These actions enable people from diverse cultures and nationalities to rapidly become part of the Abraaj metaculture.

Tips for Rapid Culture Change

- Focus on the behaviors that matter.
- Get bottom-up support and involvement.
- Model the new behavior to employees.
- Realign the reward system with desired behaviors and cultural attributes.
- Make sure that people see a clear connection between their new behaviors and business results.
- Communicate and recommunicate organizational values and the Main Thing.

The right culture is an important precondition for organizational alignment. Once attitudes, beliefs, values, and behavior are consistent with the Main Thing of the business, rapid realignment, the subject of Chapter 8, is possible.

Key Points on Culture

- Organizational culture has a documented impact on operating performance.
- Culture is the product of four dynamically related components: attitudes, beliefs, values, and behavior.
- Attitudes, beliefs, and values are deeply ingrained and difficult to change.
- The fastest and most effective way to change attitudes and beliefs is to change people's behavior and show them the beneficial results of the new behavior.
- Organizational culture is revealed in artifacts and symbols, the stories people tell, relationships, and the rituals and rules that guide behavior.

Things to Do

- Select one of your key strategic goals.
- Determine which behaviors are necessary to achieve that goal.
- Identify cultural attributes that will foster those behaviors.
- Test your conclusions.
- Ask managers how they will model and promote the key behaviors.

EIGHT

Rapid Realignment: Methods and Tools

- Alignment at the top
- Measuring current alignment at every level
- A self-diagnostic test
- Web-based systems
- Moving slow-fast-faster

If you've ever skippered a sailboat, you know that you cannot simply set a course and then sit back, relax, and watch the waves roll by. Some combination of external and internal factors will be driving your boat off course: a shift in the direction or speed of the wind, a hidden current, your force on the tiller, or something else you cannot anticipate. These disruptions require that you stay alert by keeping an eye on the compass bearing, the sails, the knot indicator, and the direction of the wind and make adjustments as needed. By sensing and responding to changes as they happen, you can keep the boat on a steady course.

Organizations have a lot in common with a sailboat. They are continually buffeted by forces that push them off course and out of alignment. Technological change, social forces, competition, and government regulation are just a few of those disruptive forces. The result is that alignment is a continual challenge for management, not something that can be set and forgotten. In their popular book *Built to Last*, Jim Collins and

Jerry Porras acknowledged that fact when they wrote, "Attaining align-ment ... is a never-ending process of identifying and doggedly correct-ing misalignment that pushes a company away from its core ideology or impedes progress." Because the pace of change is swift, management must respond with equal speed, that is, with *rapid* realignment.

Our prescription for rapid realignment has the following steps:

- Align the leadership team.
- Create an online alignment portal.
- Develop a tool to assess current alignment.
- Make periodic assessments.
- Track progress and provide feedback.

In this chapter we'll take you through the most important of those steps.

Align the Leadership Team

The first step toward rapid realignment is to get the leadership team's members aligned with the Main Thing of the enterprise and its strat-egy. If you're thinking, "Our team is already aligned; we agree on everything that matters," good for you. Unfortunately, most executives cannot say that with a straight face. The CEO of a major utility told us that he felt that most senior teams, including his, were like dys-functional families. A survey of 2,000 executives by Booz supports the dysfunctional family idea, as revealed in these disturbing findings[1]:

- 64 percent said that their company had too many conflicting priorities.
- 49 percent reported that they didn't have a list of strategic priorities.
- 54 percent reported that their employees did not understand how the company created value.

To support alignment effectively, a leadership team should be very close to 100 percent in each of these areas.

We recommend aligning leaders at an offsite meeting that accom-plishes the following:

- Agrees on the Main Thing of the business
- Defines reality in terms of what needs to change
- Creates a small number of metrics tied to the Main Thing
- Identifies and eliminates operational and cultural barriers to execution
- Develops personal 3-, 30-, and 60-day commitments to action

A Tool for Assessing Current Alignment

The old axiom "You can't manage if you can't measure" was never truer than in the context of alignment. Measurement can tell us how well an organization is performing against the things that matter, including each critical success factor. Lacking accurate measurement, a manager cannot know where or how to intervene. He or she is like a pilot whose aircraft lacks an altimeter, a compass, and an airspeed gauge. In other words, he or she is flying blind.

Every organization measures its operations in some way or in several ways: quarterly financial reports, weekly or monthly sales reports, customer surveys, annual employee workplace satisfaction surveys, and so forth. But do these methods measure the right things? The right things to measure are the activities that determine how well the organization performs with respect to its critical success factors. Are the measurements timely? Timely measurements alert management to problems before they get out of hand, while there are still opportunities to take corrective action.

In the course of writing this book we spent some time with Fred Smith, the founder and CEO of FedEx. Fred is a stickler for relevant and timely measurement and always has been. Every day he and his people receive a report that quantifies how well or poorly the company has performed in terms of on-time delivery. This is a mathematical representation of every one of the millions of transactions that took place during the last 24 hours. They call it the Service Quality Index. The daily SQI isn't one of those reports that disappear into a filing cabinet. It is something that every FedEx manager must read and respond to that day and every day. For Smith and company, the

SQI is the core set of cockpit instruments they watch and use to steer FedEx toward its Main Thing: People-Service-Profit.

We'll give you the whole story on SQI in Chapter 9, but for now the takeaway is its relevance and timeliness as a tool for alignment. A company needs both. A workplace climate survey given to employees, for instance, may be relevant for management decisions, but how timely can it be if 12 months slips away between surveys and if it takes a month or two to tally and analyze the results? Think of all the damage that can be done and the many alignment opportunities that will be missed if data are unavailable for 11 or 12 months. Rapid realignment is possible only when we know what's going on *now*—as close to real time as possible. If acquiring timely data seems an unrealistic task, remember that companies have been practicing real-time process measurement ever since the quality movement took hold. Companies that adopt quality methods are constantly measuring output quality and throughput time and comparing what they find to standards. When they detect a discrepancy, they hunt down the cause and quickly fix it. This is in effect a form of rapid realignment, though it is narrowly focused. What we advocate is a broader approach to measurement that considers the alignment of both processes and people.

It's easy to measure key process outputs. At the Farmington Bank it is the time it takes to process a loan application. Other companies track the percentage of customer orders that are filled correctly each day, the number of products returned for refunds or warranty work, and so forth. These are things we can see and touch. But how can people alignment be measured? How can we gauge employees' understanding of company strategy? How can we know if employees perceive the rewards system as supportive and aligned with the work we ask them to do? Is it possible to put a number on the level of collaboration between different units?

Yes; all these things can be done. These people aspects of alignment can be measured through standard survey methods and data analysis. "Sure," you're thinking, "we could do that, but employee surveys are time-consuming and expensive to administer. And by the time we have the results, the data will probably be outdated." Fortunately, the Internet, social media technology, and some very clever software have made it possible to tap easily and inexpensively into the employee population for the measures that matter, and they provide results the next day.

You can also design your own simple assessment tool, one that can be administered and scored manually. We'll now show you how.

A WEB-BASED ASSESSMENT TOOL

To learn more about web-based assessment systems, read the Appendix at the end of this book. There a case study describes one such system and its application to a large organization.

The web-based system we use is built around a questionnaire containing 80 to 90 normative statements. To understand how it's built and how it works, consider the short-form diagnostic tool we share with clients for that purpose. This simple version is based on 16 normative statements: statements that describe how things should be. Examples are "My manager provides coaching when I need it," "People in this organization understand our strategy," and "I have access to information about customer needs."

We suggest that you complete and score the questionnaire shown in Table 8.1, which will give you a rough measure of your organization's overall alignment. The scores you assign will reflect your personal view of organizational alignment. A more robust view is obtained when many of your colleagues and employees, preferably in other departments or units, participate in the same exercise. If others participate, calculate the *average* of their scores for each dimension of alignment. Of course, participant anonymity is essential.

Instructions for Self-Diagnosis

Table 8.1 lists four normative statements on each dimension of alignment: strategy, customers, people, and processes. Thus, there are 16 statements in all. Indicate how strongly you disagree or agree with each statement on a scale of 0 to 10, with 10 being the highest level of agreement. Then, for each set of four statements, total your numerical responses. They will fall some somewhere between 0 (total misalignment) and 40 (perfect alignment) for each dimension.

TABLE 8.1
ALIGNMENT SHORT-FORM DIAGNOSTIC

	Strongly Disagree										Strongly Agree
Strategy											
Organizational strategies are clearly communicated to me.	0	1	2	3	4	5	6	7	8	9	10
Organizational strategies guide the identification of skills and knowledge that I need.	0	1	2	3	4	5	6	7	8	9	10
People here are willing to change when new strategies require it.	0	1	2	3	4	5	6	7	8	9	10
Our senior managers agree on the organization's strategy.	0	1	2	3	4	5	6	7	8	9	10
					Total =						
Customers											
For each product or service we provide, there is an agreed-upon prioritized list of what customers care about.	0	1	2	3	4	5	6	7	8	9	10
People in this organization are given useful information about customer complaints.	0	1	2	3	4	5	6	7	8	9	10
Strategies are periodically reviewed to ensure the satisfaction of customer needs.	0	1	2	3	4	5	6	7	8	9	10
Processes are reviewed regularly to ensure that they contribute to the attainment of customer satisfaction.	0	1	2	3	4	5	6	7	8	9	10
					Total =						

People

	0	1	2	3	4	5	6	7	8	9	10
Our organization collects information from employees about how well things work.	0	1	2	3	4	5	6	7	8	9	10
My work unit or team is rewarded for its performance as a team.	0	1	2	3	4	5	6	7	8	9	10
Groups within the organization cooperate to achieve customer satisfaction.	0	1	2	3	4	5	6	7	8	9	10
When processes are changed, the impact on employee satisfaction is measured.	0	1	2	3	4	5	6	7	8	9	10

Total = ☐

Processes

	0	1	2	3	4	5	6	7	8	9	10
Our managers care about *how* work gets done as well as about the results.	0	1	2	3	4	5	6	7	8	9	10
We review our work processes regularly to see how well they are functioning.	0	1	2	3	4	5	6	7	8	9	10
When something goes wrong, we correct the underlying reasons so that the problem will not happen again.	0	1	2	3	4	5	6	7	8	9	10
Processes are reviewed to ensure that they contribute to the achievement of strategic goals.	0	1	2	3	4	5	6	7	8	9	10

Total = ☐

149

FIGURE 8. I

ALIGNMENT PROFILE

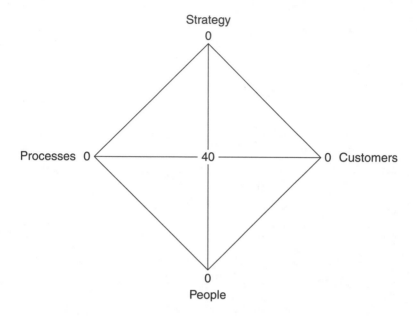

Now look at Figure 8.1, a graphic image of our alignment framework. There you will see each dimension, with 40 at dead center and 0 on the outer end of each dimension. Put a dot at the appropriate position along each dimension for each of your four totals. For example, if your total for customer alignment is 20, place a dot midway between 0 and 40 on the customer dimension. When that has been done, connect the four dots. This will give you a visual profile of your organization's current state of alignment.

In a well-aligned organization, the connected dots form a very tight pattern around the center; a poorly aligned organization has the opposite profile (see Figure 8.2).

From Analysis to Action

Both the numeric scores and the graphic profile indicate where your organization's alignment is strong and where it is weak. Remember, by restricting participation to members of your team, department, or business unit, you can focus on the unit that matters most to you. If

FIGURE 8.2

WELL-ALIGNED AND POORLY ALIGNED PROFILES

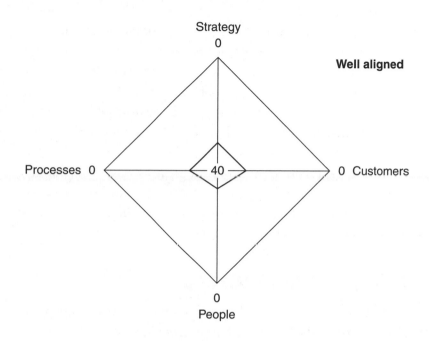

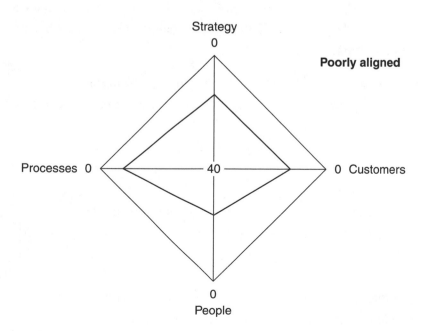

you are a manager, use information from the tool to prioritize your intervention. To further pinpoint areas of misalignment, average the scores people assigned to each question within the areas of weakness. For example, if your profile indicates poor alignment along the customer dimension, look at people's responses to the four customer questions and find which had the lowest scores. For instance, if the statement "People in this organization are given useful information about customer complaints" received extremely low ratings (0 to 3), this would signal an area for rapid corrective action on your part.

Once you've taken corrective action in areas of misalignment, give people a month or two for those corrections to take hold; then ask the same people to take the same diagnostic questionnaire. The new scores will reveal whether your intervention has been successful.

Building a Better Mousetrap

Our short-form diagnostic tool provides a rough take on alignment, but to get a truly robust and reliable view, you need to beef it up with many more normative statements. Here are some other statements used in the larger, web-based 80- to 90-statement version we use in our consulting practice:

- I can speak truthfully to anyone in this organization.
- The organization continually looks for ways to improve our access to information.
- The training offered in my unit helps me do a better job.
- I know that customer satisfaction is an important part of my daily work.
- High integrity and mutual respect are key aspects of our culture.
- I feel included in the decisions that affect my work and schedule.
- My immediate manager is passionate about making our strategy a success.
- Quality is an ever-present concern in my department.
- I know how my work contributes to the organization's strategy.

You get the picture.

A web-based system that incorporates this larger, more robust set has many advantages. With the web-based system we use, completing the survey usually takes no more than 20 minutes. The system's software instantaneously tabulates all the responses and automatically arrays them in user-friendly graphic and numeric formats. We like this system because it's capable of breaking down data by operating unit and employee demographics, making it possible to zoom down to the source of a problem. It can capture variation hidden within an average. Averages are deceptive. For example, if your head was in the oven and your feet were in the freezer, you'd be on average quite comfortable. Variation within that average tells a different story. For instance, suppose that employees on average registered an acceptable level of satisfaction with company culture. The system might, however, reveal that some employees in the customer service department were highly dissatisfied with its culture. Their dissatisfaction would be concealed by the average. With that knowledge, management can direct its attention to the customer service department.

The beauty of these software-enabled systems is that they can quickly and easily take the temperature of the organization and pinpoint areas of misalignment. Armed with data, management can intervene and employees can be engaged in making adjustments that bring things into alignment. The case study in the Appendix describes an actual application, with examples of the data displays given to management.

TIPS FOR AN EFFECTIVE ALIGNMENT WEB PORTAL

To make the most of an alignment program, we recommend a dedicated web portal through which people can access the information they need and the messages management wants to get out. The site should provide the following:

- *A video message from the CEO.* Speaking on this clip, the CEO should briefly explain the what, why, and how of the initiative: what alignment is about, why it is important and

(Continued)

being undertaken now, and how every person can be a part
of it. It's important to define reality with data and share what
needs to change and to describe the metrics that will be used
to track those changes. It's also important to describe the
behaviors that need changing.

- *A brief introduction to the alignment concept.* A website link
  should take viewers to a page that succinctly explains the
  key concepts: the Main Thing of the business, vertical and
  horizontal alignment, how alignment will be measured,
  and frequently asked questions.

- *A link to an alignment measurement questionnaire.*
  The company should develop or purchase an online
  questionnaire-based tool for measuring critical success
  factors and the current state of alignment at every level
  and for every unit. Employees should be able to access that
  questionnaire quickly and easily. Both management and
  employees should have access to the questionnaire's results
  and the current state of alignment.

- *A chat room.* Here people can share information, ideas, and
  best practices.

- *An alignment blog.* Management should appoint an
  operations person with good written communication skills
  and feet in the trenches to write a weekly blog about the
  progress of the alignment project. The blog should profile
  best practices and communicate victories, setbacks, and
  lessons learned.

The Slow-Fast-Faster Path to Realignment

Over the course of several years, we measured alignment in every
major U.S. Navy command, including battle groups and hospitals,
reaching close to 200,000 military and civilian personnel. Each
engagement provided an opportunity to refine our methods and

observe how capable leaders applied them to the challenge of alignment and organizational transformation. In each case, we learned something new and valuable. One of those capable leaders was Vice Admiral Phil Balisle, head of the Naval Sea Systems Command (NAVSEA).

NAVSEA is a huge enterprise with over 54,000 people and a budget of more than $24 billion. It is responsible for the technical and engineering support and the long-term maintenance of the surface fleet and submarines. It has two major business areas: shipyards for (primarily) nuclear vessel repair, with about 20,000 people, and nine warfare centers whose job is to do technical development for the many systems aboard naval ships and submarines. A third element of NAVSEA is its headquarters unit, most of which is located in Washington, D.C., with approximately 4,500 people. That unit oversees the command and houses technical expertise, which the Navy calls "technical authority."

Vice Admiral Balisle took command in 2002, at a time when the Navy's brass felt that NAVSEA needed to revolutionize its procedures, streamline operations, and break away from its perceived dedication to the status quo. Balisle shared that feeling. His experience, however, led him to believe that real, enduring change in the Navy takes a long time, especially in units as large and diverse as his new command. He also knew that the Navy's usual three-year command cycle would make implementing long-term change difficult. Could he get it all done in three years? If he succeeded, would the changes stick after he moved on?

Adding to the challenge was the fact that the majority of his workforce was civilian, not military. Most had been at their jobs for years and had developed an entrenched way of doing things that had made them resistant to change.

In taking on his task, Balisle adopted what we call a slow-fast-faster approach: taking his time initially to listen, learn, gather data, and plan; speeding up with a set of ambitious initiatives; and, finally, going all out to engage the workforce in enduring change.

Slow

With his three-year clock ticking down, Balisle knew that success would require him to take action, but he didn't immediately leap into the fray. Instead, he talked with people. He invited us in to assess the current state of alignment with our web-based tool. He brought together panels of leaders and technical experts—including experienced people from outside his command—to sort things out and plan for the future. Slowly but deliberately he used the first six months of his tenure to identify the changes he wanted to make on his watch. That would leave him two and one-half years for implementation.

Collaboration would be essential. NAVSEA was a de facto holding company of independent entities, each with its own workforce and political guardians. Even a vice admiral couldn't impose his ideas. On the bright side, Balisle was pleased to discover through our alignment assessment that he had more buy-in for realignment among senior leaders than he had anticipated.

Fast

After six months of thinking, learning, planning, and engaging others, the admiral picked up the pace, launching transformative initiatives in four key areas:

- The headquarters and program executive officers, the people who oversaw the specialized development of systems such as radar.
- Shipyards and warfare centers. Personnel were asked: What should we start doing, stop doing, or continue doing to better execute our mission? Twelve thousand responses were submitted. Those responses touched off an explosion of process improvements and workplace efficiencies.
- Service units: contracting, financial management, planning, human systems integration, accounting, supply, and logistics. A search for efficiencies began.
- People processes. How were people being managed, recruited, trained? Were the right people in the right jobs?

A fifth initiative addressed lean/Six Sigma implementation through the command.

Each initiative followed a consistent approach and involved a study team with two components: staff personnel who would be responsible for implementation and well-credentialed people who were not part of the organization and not wedded to current practices. Each initiative adopted what Balisle's teams would call a "hundred-day march." One hundred days to align and transform long-established practices seemed daunting, but Balisle felt that the foundation of change had to be laid quickly. The first 30 days of each march would be devoted to defining the problem and the objective. What needed fixing, and how could they fix it? For each initiative the remaining 70 days would be devoted to implementation. By the end of the hundred days, the goal was to have new and aligned structures in place.

Faster

The balance of Balisle's years in the command were devoted to making those new structures enduring and engaging the workforce—from top to bottom—in the new way of operating. Gaining buy-in was an important challenge for each team. It required an aggressive communication plan that would reach every sailor and civilian employee with a consistent message over time. As in every other successful example of rapid realignment, message consistency and repetition were required to sustain the alignment initiative. Measurement was also essential. Balisle and his team used our web-based alignment assessment tool each year to measure how people were responding to changes and to identify barriers to further progress.

As challenging as the NAVSEA project was, and as taxing as its hundred-day marches were for people, it worked. As Phil Balisle told us:

> We saw results very quickly—money savings and improved
> efficiencies. We were doing jobs with less people, were
> cleaning up work areas so people felt better about their
> work and the organization of it. We could see tangible

things that were very important to where we had to go.
We also received recognition of progress in the federal
government's 2005 survey of Best Places to Work, which
showed significant improvement in NAVSEA across-the-
board scores and a rating well above Navy and Department
of Defense averages. These results, which included ranking
number one in effective leadership among U.S. Navy
organizations, were an especially notable achievement
given the amount of change we imposed on the workforce.

These scores were gratifying, as NAVSEA had consistently ranked low
in the Department of Defense survey prior to Balisle's command.

The notion of going slow at the beginning of a change or realignment
initiative, as Phil Balisle did, doesn't appeal to many executives, particularly when they're faced with big problems. Executives, after all,
are action-oriented people, and when they're new to a job, people
expect to see things happening quickly. Nevertheless, the wisdom of
starting slowly, gathering facts, talking to people, testing ideas with
others, enlisting support, and mapping out a way forward has been
confirmed again and again. One of our favorite examples of this is the
case of Ingar Skaug, who was recruited in 1990 to lead Wilhelmsen
Lines, a Norway-based global shipping company.[2]

Skaug's move to Wilhelmsen Lines was triggered by tragedy.
A plane carrying 50 senior managers and staff people had crashed,
killing all aboard. In addition to the pain of this loss, the company had
experienced years of financial troubles and was barely profitable.

Ingar Skaug, then vice president and deputy chief operating officer of the Norwegian segment of the Scandinavian Air System, came
to his new position some six months after the plane crash, and he
came as a true outsider who had to learn the fundamentals of that
business, acquaint himself with its personnel, and steer the company
into a new and better direction.

The new CEO saw many challenges at Wilhelmsen. Grief per-
vaded the organization. The company's culture was very traditional

and formal, with a centralized decision-making process and little teamwork or organizational learning. In addition, the IT system was outdated and employees were more focused on shipping vessels than on customers. Skaug, in contrast, viewed creative, motivated, and empowered people as the key to business success.

Shortly after his arrival, Skaug began a series of discussions with the company's top 20–25 people with the goal of establishing a shared set of values and business principles. With core beliefs centered on empowerment and engagement, Skaug was always open to input and dialogue, and he traveled the globe, meeting key customers, conducting employee seminars and meetings with all employees at each major office. Employees were surveyed about the organization's climate, culture, values, and working relationships.

Months went by, and the new CEO still hadn't announced any major changes. People began to wonder, "When is he going to do something?" Some asked that question to his face. But while Ingar Skaug appeared to be doing very little, he was actually sorting out the business, building personal relationships, gathering facts, and planning his move. That move came six months after his arrival and a full year after the accident, when he shifted from slow to fast, after a heartfelt recognition and ceremony that commemorated the tragedy.

A believer in the value of organizational development, the new CEO launched a formal coaching process for managers. He initiated customer surveys in a quest for external feedback about the company's strengths and weaknesses. And to better integrate his poorly aligned enterprise, he began a campaign to articulate values, establish goals, develop clear strategies, and tap the human capital at his disposal. He firmly believed that these actions would create a climate of engaged, empowered employees and—eventually—better operating results. His leadership story is a testimony to the power of alignment and demonstrates, once again, the relationship between alignment and business results.

As the result of his efforts, the company grew significantly over the years. By the time he moved on to become CEO of the Wilhelmsen Group, the company had reached annual revenues of $1.3 billion, with over 3,000 worldwide employees transporting 1.5 million cars and 300,000 "roll-on/roll-off" units of vehicle cargo per year in over 70 world-class vessels. When we asked Skaug what happened to the Wilhelmsen Group after he became Group CEO, he said "When I retired we had 142 vessels, a revenue more like $3–5 billion, 23,000 employees, and 475 offices in 79 countries, servicing 2,200 ports in the world with maritime services. We also built an integrated logistics capability for vehicles and heavy machinery."

Postscript: On retiring from active management in 2010, Ingar Skaug became the Chairman of the Center for Creative Leadership, after serving as a board member since 1991, the longest-serving board member in the Center's history. Skaug also received the 2010 Marion F. Gislason Award from the Executive Development Roundtable at Boston University in recognition of his achievements as a leader and for his lifetime contributions to the field of leadership and leadership development.

Key Points on Tools and Methods

- Organization alignment should begin with the leadership team.
- A web-based assessment tool supported by an intranet portal can measure alignment quickly and often.
- Don't rush. Use a slow-fast-faster approach to realignment and transformation.

Things to Do

- Take and score the self-diagnostic questionnaire in Table 8.1 to get a rough idea of your current level of alignment.
- Map your alignment scores on the alignment framework in Figure 8.1. Where are you well-aligned or misaligned?
- Get a more accurate assessment by asking others in your organization to do the same.

NINE

The Enterprise Effect: The Ultimate Expression of Alignment

Partnering as a precursor to the Enterprise Effect

Two independent hospitals create a virtual enterprise

Competing collectively, operating independently, and managing collaboratively at FedEx

Two naval commands learn to operate as one

The unique behaviors of enterprise leadership

We hope that you now share our enthusiasm for the concept of rapid alignment and its methods. Bringing all the people, the processes, and the strategy of an enterprise into rapid alignment with one another and with customers is in our experience the very best way to assure exceptional organizational performance. But, you may ask, can alignment be applied to the more complex organizations that many executives now lead: joint ventures, corporations formed from multiple acquisitions, and informal collaborations that address a common mission? Our answer is an emphatic yes. But a different kind of leadership, which we call Big Hat leadership, is required.

The cases in this chapter should provide encouragement to readers who struggle with misalignment and subpar performance in those complex situations. Each case demonstrates how metric-driven management, attention to culture, and putting customers first can pull diverse and independent operations together to the point where they think and act as one entity on behalf of a single Main Thing, creating a "virtual enterprise" that provides, from the customer's perspective, a seamless experience and a single brand. We call this unique state of peak performance the *Enterprise Effect*. Creating and maintaining it may be today's greatest leadership challenge, but as our cases indicate, it can be achieved through alignment, and the results are well worth the effort.

Partnering as a First Step

Partnering is the first step on the way to the Enterprise Effect. By showing one face to their common customers and by making their processes and systems seamless in service to those customers, two parties can create greater value for customers—and for themselves.

As was noted in Chapter 5, each supplier-customer interaction represents an opportunity for the supplier to learn more about the customer's requirements and gain feedback about how well or poorly he or she is meeting those requirements. In a truly aligned organization, that learning is quickly reflected in process improvements. Partnering takes the supplier-customer relationship to a new and deeper level, helping to improve both parties' work processes and sharing successes. The following five questions help partners work together more effectively:

1. What do you *really* need from me?
2. What do you do with what I provide you?
3. Are there gaps between what I give you and what you need?

4. What problems might I help you with?

5. Am I providing things you *don't* need?

Answering these questions will help you and your business partners help yourselves. Take the example of a company producing natural gas, with over 900 wells. Since gas is a commodity product, supplier-customer discussions revolved almost entirely around price. The gas company's president wondered if there was a way to break out of that constrictive situation.

In speaking with one of his major customers, a utility company, he learned that gas storage accounted for some of that customer's highest costs. He asked, "If I can change my processes to deliver gas in ways that will reduce your high storage costs, will you pay me an above-market price for it?" The utility was agreeable, and the math worked out favorably for both parties. The gas company repeated this win-win arrangement with each of its larger customers.

In this case, a supplier and a customer partnered for mutual benefit. Let's take this partnering concept to the next level: creating greater value for the customer's customer for the benefit of all the parties.

We learned the importance of the concept of the customer's customer early in our work with Walmart and Procter & Gamble. Walmart founder Sam Walton and John Pepper, then president of P&G, wanted to build a closer business relationship. Duplication of effort and imperfect coordination were costing each company millions of dollars each year. At one meeting, Walton surprised everyone by asking the P&G people to explain their processes for supplying his stores. The P&G people were at first reluctant to reveal their processes but agreed to do so when Walmart agreed to do the same thing. The processes that P&G shared included new product development, marketing and sales, manufacturing, shipping, and billing. For its part, Walmart shared its purchasing, merchandising, supply chain management, and pricing processes.

Victor, who was facilitating the meeting, took them a step further. He suggested that they define the needs of their shared customers: Walmart shoppers. To do that, he organized the 30-some senior managers from the two organizations into small mixed teams. Their job was to report what their customers cared most about and their respective business strategies. The participants quickly realized that the two giant companies had very different ideas about the needs of their ultimate customers. In Walmart's view, customers wanted everyday low prices with no sales, no promotions, and no coupons. P&G saw consumers as wanting special deals and promotions. These very different perspectives explained in part why the two companies were failing to optimize their relationship in service of their customers. Through dialogue, the two parties agreed to a number of policy and process changes that would better align their efforts and deliver greater value to Walmart shoppers.

Postscript: The Walmart–P&G partnering effort resulted in a 300 percent increase in P&G sales through the giant retailer over 18 months.

We had a similar experience with a major European home goods manufacturer and representatives of a key retailer. The manufacturer's representatives were from production, product design, marketing, and sales and came from several countries. The purpose of the meeting was to communicate the retailer's understanding of its customers to the manufacturer, improve product development to better meet consumer needs across national boundaries, and help the retailer better communicate the distinctive value of the manufacturer's product line. The task was complicated by the fact that the retailer operated in different countries, where customers had different cultural attributes. As in the P&G–Walmart case, greater understanding between the parties led to improved processes for serving the customer's customers.

Postscript: Tighter horizontal alignment led to a new business model for doing business within and across borders. Sales increased dramatically, and product returns, a growing problem, were significantly reduced.

Tips for Partnering with External and Internal Customers

- Bring customers into your organization to meet face to face with people other than salespeople.
- Use social media technology to link internal functions with external customers.
- Ensure that meetings whose purpose is to improve processes include representatives from the affected functions.
- Map each major process's value chain to identify internal suppliers and customers. Then bring them together with the goal of better understanding each party's requirements and finding out how each can add greater value.
- Schedule meetings that bring together your external customers and their customers.

Beyond Partnering: The Enterprise Effect

Some organizations go beyond partnering to create a virtual organization dedicated to providing greater value to end customers. In doing this they have reached the ultimate expression of alignment, which we call the Enterprise Effect. The three cases that follow demonstrate the Enterprise Effect in action. Here, separate entities seamlessly combine their resources and capabilities, unleash synergies, and create a single face for the marketplace. And everyone benefits. The following questions will help you achieve the Enterprise Effect:

- Who are our common customers, and what do they value?
- How can we, acting together, create greater value for our common customers?
- How can we make each other successful?

Dana-Farber/Children's Hospital Cancer Center

The designation of Dana-Farber/Children's Hospital Cancer Center (DF/CHCC) as the number one pediatric cancer center was not the result of the happy coincidence of the physical proximity of a world-class cancer research center with a world-class children's hospital. Indeed, the two institutions had been collaborating in pediatric cancer care for years. Two separate institutions, two separate boards, two separate Harvard medical faculties.

Dana-Farber is one of the world's most advanced cancer research and treatment centers. Approximately 300,000 patients from around the world visit it annually for treatment or to participate in clinical trials. It is internationally renowned for combining research and clinical excellence. The institute's expertise in these two aspects of the fight against cancer uniquely positions it to develop and test the next generation of cancer therapies.

Children's Hospital Boston, affiliated with Harvard Medical School, is situated nearby. Children's Hospital is widely recognized as one of the nation's top pediatric care facilities. As an independent, large pediatric medical center, it offers a complete range of healthcare services for children and young people through 21 years of age. In a typical year, its medical staff handles approximately half a million outpatient cases, 60,000 emergency room visits, and 25,000 inpatient surgeries. Children's Hospital is also home to the world's largest research enterprise based at a pediatric hospital.

For more than 60 years these two great medical institutions, acting individually, have provided care to pediatric cancer patients. Dana-Farber provided outpatient care, and Children's Hospital provided all of the inpatient care. But it was only after the formation of the Dana-Farber/Children's Hospital Cancer Center that they came to be recognized as the nation's premier pediatric cancer center. This is an interesting organizational arrangement in that each institution has its own board of directors and executive leaders, its own staff of Harvard Medical School clinicians and researchers, its own facilities and fund-raising, and so forth. Each conducts its own strategy planning. To complicate things further, some Dana-Farber physicians are academic leaders at Children's (chairs and chiefs). Each operates independently except in areas in which their capabilities in the field of pediatric cancer care intersect (Figure 9.1). At that intersection they operate as a "virtual" enterprise. DF/CHCC has no common physical plant and few jointly employed medical staff, yet it brings the best available cancer care to children.

Keeping the leadership and staff of these two separate institutions aligned with the goals of the joint enterprise and its patients seemed to us an unusual challenge. With so many chores to handle on behalf of their own institutions, what motivated their CEOs and medical professionals to insist on the very best medical practice in the jointly run venture? To find the answers, we interviewed Dr. James Mandell, the CEO of Children's; Dr. Ed Benz, Dana-Farber's CEO; and Sandra Fenwick, president and COO of Children's. What we heard from them merits repeating here as these healthcare executives have mastered the art of alignment in a virtual enterprise.

FIGURE 9.1

THE BEST CANCER CARE FOR CHILDREN

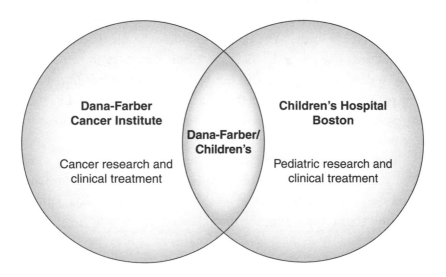

Both CEOs are products of Harvard Medical School, training and education, but the two men are very different in temperament and specialty training. Dr. Mandell is a highly regarded urological surgeon, whereas Dr. Benz, a self-described "gene jockey," is a renowned researcher. Although they became CEOs at approximately the same time, they had not known each other before returning to Boston from leadership positions elsewhere. The DF/CHCC situation they manage is complicated. Some Dana-Farber physicians, for example, are leaders at the academic level at Children's Hospital (co-chiefs). Each hospital carries out strategic planning and fund-raising independently.

The two CEOs recognized early in their tenures that their institutions had to be more clinically and strategically aligned if joint operations were to attain the highest level of medical performance and compete at the national and international level. Even though they represented two excellent organizations, they felt the clinical care system for pediatric cancer care was not as good as it could be. By improving clinical care, they reasoned, they would also inform and improve medical research. The challenge was finding a way to structure, align, and build an enterprise that would fulfill that aspiration.

The customer voice as represented by the patient advisory committee, which consisted of parents and patients at Dana-Farber, gave alignment a big push. Committee members asked the two CEOs, "Why do patients have to register three times? Why must they have two separate ID cards? Why doesn't Children's know when a patient has had the same test at Dana-Farber? This is no way to run a business." Indeed, misalignment in the hospital systems forced patients and patient families to jump through needless hoops. As Dr. Benz explained, "There was a Dana-Farber way, a Children's way, and [once alignment was achieved] a reconciliation way."

To achieve greater alignment, the two CEOs saw a need for a cultural change from a largely research orientation to one that recognized the critical importance of all three missions: teaching, clinical care, and research. Getting the medical staff to buy into that change would not be easy, as most of the staff didn't recognize that the system was broken and not working as well as it could for patients.

When we asked how they changed the culture, Dr. Mandell replied, "We stood shoulder to shoulder in demonstrating our commitment to changing practice patterns, the recognition system, the recruitment strategy, and so forth." The two organizations began, for example, to conduct joint strategic planning, as distinct from past practice; each partner presented its plans to the other for comment. They also unified the leadership structure of DF/CHCC. The director of pediatric oncology at Dana-Farber and the chief of hematology/oncology at Children's Hospital formed a unified team, acting as coleaders in both organizations and the joint enterprise. A joint marketing program was established. Care was taken to assure that the personal perks and status of staff members would not be jeopardized by their participation in the virtual enterprise. Regular meetings between administrative and academic leaders—for example, between COOs and physician leaders—helped solve current and prospective problems. The unique cultures of clinical practice and medical research began communicating effectively for the first time.

Alignment within DF/CHCC was initially maintained by the close and collaborative relationship between the two CEOs. Both men realized, however, that being linked at the top would be insufficient, that the joint effort would pull apart in the absence of "subcutaneous stitches from the ground level up." That knitting together was achieved as people adopted new ways of working together and as systems became more and more seamlessly integrated. Sandra Fenwick gave us some tangible examples of those subcutaneous stitches.

The DF/CHCC enterprise of today had its beginnings in activities that started before Drs. Mandell and Benz assumed their roles. As Sandra Fenwick explained to us, both institutions had been working on improving processes between them. They also formed a limited liability company, which provided the legal framework for the pediatric cancer center.

> It started with a clinical event that involved a problem with order entry for chemotherapy. We put a joint committee together from both institutions to explore better ways for

clinicians to order drugs. We discovered that there was nothing on the market specifically designed for pediatric cancer patients. So we built our own. We put a team together of clinicians and IT people and decided to split the costs 50/50. It was a multimillion-dollar commitment, and we looked at it through the eyes of the patient. It was basically the first project we decided to do together.

When Jim and Ed came on board we began looking at joint marketing, joint quality, and joint palliative care programs, all viewed through the perspective of what's best for the patient. We never discussed which party would have the greater benefit. We just kept the 50/50 split. At that time, the corporate structures were different. The finances were separate. So these kinds of decisions were very important. The goal was to get people's heads around the idea of a joint patient care program.

Physician leadership needed to stress the clinical needs of patients first, above teaching or research. Simultaneously they had to get nursing on the same page; they had to share common standards, common approaches to patients, and common protocols.

A Dana-Farber physician was made clinical director of the joint program at both institutions. The same thing happened in nursing. The vice president of medical nursing at Children's Hospital was made joint head of nursing of both the outpatient clinic at Dana-Farber as well as inpatient care at Children's Hospital. As Sandra Fenwick explained, "We split her salary, and she ended up with a dual reporting relationship to the chief nursing officers at both hospitals. We tried to break through some of the structural issues of reporting and employment and the like, and said, 'Let's just make this work with a common program.'"

Collaboration was manifested in many ways during subsequent years. When Children's decided to recruit a new chief of the Division of Hematology/Oncology, it did so with input from the Dana-Farber leadership. That new head at Children's Hospital was instrumental in emphasizing clinical research and clinical trials, which led to the recruitment of a chief of clinical trials. Shared funding, to the tune of $6 million, provided the infrastructure for those important clinical trials.

"We had to look at every component of vision, leadership, and investment," Fenwick told us, "and ask, 'Is this the best it can be?' Jim and Ed were very supportive of the decisions that followed."

Nevertheless, the two leaders recognized that their personal involvement, even down to small operational issues and the problems of their academic leaders, remained necessary. Their involvement focused on making the lives of the faculty better, just as the faculty's responsibility was to improve the lives of patients. As Dr. Mandell put it, "If you don't get involved, it won't stick. But you also have to put in structures that deliver."

Still, change for DF/CHCC took time. When we mentioned our term *rapid realignment*, both CEOs chuckled, noting that they were affiliated with an organization (Harvard) that "had not moved rapidly in over 300 years." Dr. Benz also noted that in their business, especially medical education, people who try to do revolutionary things fail. "You succeed," he said, "with evolutionary things."

More recently a "gang of eight" was formed. It consisted of the two CEOs, two COOs, and four senior physicians who held leadership appointments at each institution. Its purpose was to provide a consistent, Big Hat leadership message throughout the enterprise. A separate, board that includes the CEO and two trustees from each organization continues from its original LLC founding.

Challenges remain. Leadership is tackling the issues of separate billing for the services provided to patients as well as enhanced marketing and joint fund-raising for the enterprise. But the Main Thing of providing the world's best comprehensive cancer center for children continues to align both institutions. Sandra Fenwick summarized the most critical element in the creation of an enterprise when she told us, "One of the biggest issues that needed to be overcome was the issue of trust. Having people build a common vision, understanding what the external threats and opportunities were, commit the required resources, and build trust at every level is absolutely essential. People had to say, 'This isn't Children's Hospital or Dana-Farber—this is the Center.'"

Postscript: *U.S. News & World Report* ranked Children's Hospital Boston and Dana-Farber Cancer Institute as the top pediatric cancer hospitals in the United States in its 2011–2012 Best Children's Hospitals guide.

FedEx

If you're like us, you have been wowed again and again by the quality service you receive from FedEx. Whether it's an urgent overnight delivery, a special gift you had shipped at low cost from an online retailer, a heavy forklift for which you needed day-specific delivery, or an important print job done quickly at FedEx Office, you have to be impressed by this company's ability to get it right the first time—again and again and again.

It didn't start out auspiciously. On its first day in business in 1971, the company shipped 14 items, and every one of them arrived late. But on the day we visited FedEx's Memphis headquarters in late 2011 to interview founder/CEO Fred Smith, the company had shipped 17 million items, and only a minuscule percentage had failed to arrive on time. Customers are not the only ones who are happy; shareholders have done very well, and FedEx is consistently rated as one of the best U.S. companies to work for. *Fortune* ranks it among its top 10 Most Admired Companies.

FedEx has a single public face but is actually an enterprise with many mission-oriented units.[1] Its core companies are FedEx Express, FedEx Ground, FedEx Freight, and FedEx Services. The FedEx umbrella also covers "specialty" companies such as FedEx Office, formerly Kinko's; FedEx Trade Networks, which handles ocean freight; and FedEx SmartPost, which has become one of the corporation's fastest growing operations by working with the U.S. Postal Service. Each has a different mission and operates with substantial independence. Each has its own CEO and board of internal executives. And each operating unit, along with every employee, is bound together by what they call the Purple Promise: "I will make every FedEx experience outstanding." To keep that promise, each employee knows that he or she must do the following:

- Do whatever it takes to satisfy our customers.

- Always treat customers in a professional, competent, polite, and caring manner.

- Handle every transaction with the precision required to achieve the highest-quality service.

- Process all customer information with 100 percent accuracy.

The Purple Promise gives everyone—from the C-suite down to the sorting line and the delivery truck—an internal guidance system. Any time an executive, a manager, or a rank-and-file team member confronts a situation that demands a decision (What should I do?), the Purple Promise steers him or her toward the right choice.

Naturally, it takes more than a motivational slogan to keep a multi-company business aligned and acting as one, in a quality way, with a single face presented to the public. FedEx relies on three mechanisms to achieve that alignment and capture the Enterprise Effect: a culture of measurement, adherence to a common methodology of quality assurance, and an overarching operating strategy.

A Culture of Measurement

In our many years of consulting we've never encountered an enterprise that is as dedicated to performance measurement as FedEx. For more than the two decades of our work with the company, FedEx has taken daily measures of customer satisfaction, loyalty, and transactional quality. These measures are tallied within a composite score called the Service Quality Index (SQI).

The SQI is a fundamental feature of the FedEx culture and part of its DNA. SQI captures the quality of millions of daily transactions as experienced by customers: delivery and pickup reliability, shipment integrity, lost freight, tracking accuracy, and timelines. Says FedEx's Senior Vice President of Global Communications William Margaritas, "We've always measured our daily transactions because they indicate where we can improve efficiency, keep costs low, and keep service levels high. More important, the SQI we use today has been broadened to give management more information on the customer experience across the spectrum of touch points: the sales interface, the customer service center, driver/courier contact, billing, FedEx.com, shipping, and so forth." Some measures, he points out, are quantitative, whereas others—especially those which gauge loyalty and customer feelings about the company—are qualitative in nature. This broader understanding of customer sentiment, he told us, has become more important as FedEx has expanded its portfolio of services beyond the one-trick pony of overnight delivery.

Greater concern with how FedEx is perceived by customers has also resulted in gathering what the company calls "reputational intelligence."[2] Reputation, as they see it, is distinct from brand yet complementary to it. For the company, reputation is a valued asset, one capable of instilling trust, admiration, and respect in all stakeholders, including employees. Employees of a high-reputation company become its ambassadors and behave in ways that uphold that reputation—and the brand.

In light of its dedication to measurement, we were not surprised to learn that FedEx measures its reputation. Periodic audits probe each "pillar" of the company's reputation as perceived by stakeholders: emotional appeal, product and service offerings, financial performance, social responsibility, the workplace environment, vision, and leadership. Management uses audit results to better understand the components of the company's reputation and create strategies for increasing its "reputational capital."

Fred Smith once told us that SQI and other key metrics are like the airspeed, altitude, and attitude indicators on one of his company's aircraft, telling him when FedEx is in or out of trim and where he must take corrective actions: "If we manage against them every day, we'll hit our goals." He wasn't exaggerating when he said "every day." At the beginning of every business day, an SQI report card is calculated and delivered to the leadership and each of the company's operating managers. It tells them where operations are on target and where they're falling short. Managers pay attention because their individual performance ratings and bonuses are linked to the SQI of their domains.

These executives and managers are on the receiving end of another metric, the Leadership Index (LI), which measures the quality of leadership as experienced and reported by employees through periodic surveys. The LI metric helps the enterprise deliver on its policy of "guaranteed fair treatment" to all employees.

Unit-Specific Critical Success Factors and Metrics   Wisely, Fred Smith and his colleagues do not impose the same measurements on their different operating companies. Each of those companies has a unique set of customers, offers unique services, and often faces unique opportunities and competitive challenges. As Fred Smith told us:

> The imperatives of FedEx Ground are different than those of FedEx Express. . . . FedEx Ground is absolutely focused on efficiency and low-cost, day-certain delivery. FedEx Express is focused on getting the item there [fast] because there's a consequence of this item not getting there on time. And FedEx Freight is about industrial efficiency. FedEx Office, which offers document printing, copying, and binding, is different from these. You have to manage these within the overall culture but have it specifically adapted to the market segment that it is serving.

He accounts for these differences through an appropriate set of critical success factors and related performance metrics for each company. Many of those factors and metrics are common across FedEx, but others are unique. For instance, as shown in Table 9.1, the ground package business maintains the following CSFs and key metrics, among others:

TABLE 9. 1	
FEDEX GROUND	
Critical Success Factors	**Key Metrics**
• Enhance customer experience at all touch points • Improve employee and contractor satisfaction • Increase workforce diversity • Meet or exceed SQI performance goals • Protect and enhance the FedEx brand	• Optimal customer experience • Employee attitude survey • On-time service • Revenue • Operating profit • Total cost per package

These factors reflect the particular challenges and dynamics of the ground package delivery company. FedEx Freight, in contrast, uses CSFs and metrics appropriate to a business that offers priority and economical less-than-truckload delivery and makes use of many independent contractors. Again, those shown in Table 9.2 are just a handful of a larger list of this company's CSFs and metrics.

Although measuring systems are common across all FedEx companies, some metrics are weighted differently or focus on factors that are appropriate to a particular operating company. "But," says CEO Smith, "they are very powerful alignment tools."

Quality Assurance Methodologies

There is abundant variety among FedEx's operating companies. A next-day delivery system for letters and packages, for example, requires different capabilities and processes than does an operation that handles on-demand printing (FedEx Office). Nevertheless, none of the units within the broader enterprise are so different that they cannot benefit from the same quality assurance methodologies. Thus, every FedEx business uses Quality Driven Management and its process improvement methodology.

Using the same methodologies helps knit FedEx's units together. Training everyone in the same methods of quality and process

TABLE 9.2 FEDEX FREIGHT	
Critical Success Factors	**Key Metrics**
• Maintain a motivated, independent workforce • Maintain the highest level of service and customer satisfaction • Provide increasing value and transit choice for customers • Deploy competitively superior IT solutions • Protect and enhance the FedEx brand	• SQI • Customer satisfaction • On-time service • Employee turnover • Money-back guarantee refunds/ credits • DOT preventable accidents • Lost time injuries • Shipment levels

improvement has created a common language that everyone understands and a set of tools that everyone knows how to use. Thus, when the SQI or another metric reveals a problem, it can be diagnosed and discussed with terms and techniques that everyone understands.

Operating Strategy

The third mechanism that keeps this multibusiness enterprise aligned is an operating strategy that is broad enough to embrace the expanse of FedEx's operations around the world. That strategy works on three tracks:

1. *Compete collectively.* FedEx's many businesses stand out as a single worldwide brand and speak to the public with one voice.
2. *Operate independently.* Each operating unit has its own CEO, management team, and network of customers and suppliers, yet each delivers the high level of quality that customers expect.
3. *Manage collaboratively.* The independent units work together to sustain loyal relationships with employees, customers, and investors.

The strategic management committee, headed by Fred Smith and inclusive of all operating company CEOs, meets every Friday to review how well the enterprise as a whole is performing against its operating strategy. It also reviews unit-specific business performance, considers new opportunities, and stays on top of the all-important SQI.

Taken together, a culture of measurement, enterprisewide adoption of quality methods, and a common operation strategy at every layer of management have created an Enterprise Effect that keeps FedEx's confederation of independent companies and subunits acting as one.

The Naval Aviation Enterprise

There's a lot of distance between the world of hospitals, the world of package delivery, and the world of sailors and carrier jet jockeys. However, their respective leaders inevitably run up against a common challenge: getting people who identify with their individual skills or functions to raise their sights and work toward a common objective. We found a good example of leaders overcoming that challenge in the U.S. Navy.

George Labovitz and his colleagues spent four years measuring the state of alignment within major commands of the Navy and working with senior leaders to improve it, often with dramatic results. One of their assignments involved the two large organizations responsible for Naval Aviation.

Naval Aviation is one of the world's largest technical enterprises, involving over 180,000 military and civilian personnel, 3,800 aircraft, and 11 nuclear aircraft carriers. Though few outside the Navy were aware of it at the time, this war-fighting enterprise was fraying at the edges in the years just before 9/11. A high percentage of its aircraft were nonoperational at any given time, and wear and tear was taking a toll on the rest. The traditional remedy—a larger budget— was not politically feasible. What Naval Aviation needed—and what it eventually got—was an alignment-driven makeover that restored its vitality and ability to fulfill its mission and, as a bonus, returned billions of dollars to taxpayers. It is called the Naval Aviation Enterprise (NAE).

As in the Dana-Farber/Children's Hospital case, NAE's transformation involved two thoughtful and effective leaders. Together, they provided the affirmative energy needed to change their organizations and achieve outstanding results. Two senior Navy leaders, Vice Admiral Wally Massenburg and Vice Admiral Jim Zortman, waged a transformative campaign to obtain better results at lower cost from the two largest stovepipe organizations tasked with supplying the U.S. fleet with aircraft, equipment, and mission-ready people.

Wally Massenburg's Naval Air Systems Command (NAVAIR) was responsible for acquiring, testing, supplying, and repairing the Navy's aircraft and aircraft systems. For this task he had a $26 billion budget and approximately 24,000 personnel, the majority being civilians. Jim Zortman's command, Naval Air Forces, was approximately the same size but mostly was composed of military personnel. His job was to "man, train, and equip" aircraft carriers with the pilots and munitions they needed. Historically, these two huge stand-alone organizations respected each other's responsibilities but seldom coordinated on behalf of the ultimate mission. Instead, each was incentivized to optimize its activities at the expense of the other.

With the support and encouragement of their boss, Chief of Naval Operations Admiral Vern Clark, Massenburg and Zortman formed the Naval Aviation Enterprise, a virtual organization that acted as if the two separate commands were one. This phantom entity had no buildings, no budget, and no assigned personnel, yet it functioned as though it had them all. The NAE did have its own board of directors, with Zortman serving as CEO and Massenburg as COO—titles familiar to businesspeople but virtually unknown in the military. As its Main Thing this virtual enterprise adopted a single customer-focused metric: "aviation units ready for tasking at reduced cost, now and in the future." Guided by that measurable goal, the two separate organizations began operating as one and in the process doubled the availability of the fleet's combat-ready aircraft even as they reduced total personnel headcount and costs, producing multi-billion-dollar savings to taxpayers.

Massenburg is quick to point out that the NAE's success was due in part to Admiral Clark's careful succession planning and the use of what he called "strategic experiments" or pilots. Previous heads of Naval Aviation appointed by Admiral Clark—"Air Bosses"—allowed the transformation to evolve to the point where VADMs Zortman and Massenburg were able to take the concept forward. Massenburg explained:

> The first Air Boss, VADM John Nathman, didn't conceive of the enterprise concept, but supported experimenting with new ways of operating. His successor, VADM Mike Malone, developed the demand signal, i.e., readiness properly measured, and Jim Zortman took that part of the equation to a different level. The evolution of the NAE was a true team effort.

NAE's success is particularly compelling in that it took place in an environment generally hostile to change and improvement: government. Few sectors are more in need of alignment and the Enterprise Effect and more resistant to it. Government functions are usually supply-driven, and its operating units are often insular and bureaucratic. Their focus is on spending budgets and on activities versus customer-related performance metrics. That is why this example of transformation is so powerful: if the Enterprise Effect can be created in government, it can happen anywhere.

Achieving the Enterprise Effect requires radically different leadership behavior, cultural realignment, and a set of values that places the greater good above parochial ends. What is required to make this happen? Wally Massenburg shared with us his lessons learned, which we feel apply to any situation in which leaders are searching for the synergy that can make one plus one equal three, or four, or five:

- *Identify the new entity and assign a single process owner.* Whether you are bringing people from a single organization together, joining separate activities within an organization, or joining two or more disparate organizations (as in a merger), the boundaries of dollars, people, resources, and intellectual capital must be identified within the existing organizations. Assign a leader who will be responsible, accountable, and replaceable if necessary.

- *Assemble the right enterprise team and gain commitment.* Only those functional and line leaders who bring dollars, people, "stuff," and intellectual capital should be included in the decision-making enterprise team.
- *Support a single customer-driven metric that represents the Main Thing.* There must be agreement on the scope, output, and linked metrics that drive all activities in support of the Main Thing. This metric can change over time as the enterprise team becomes more confident and sophisticated in understanding the enterprise environment. This allows for continuous process improvement.
- *Agree on desired output.* Gain agreement and a shared value proposition that will focus team activities.
- *Operate with discipline, governance, and a regular drumbeat.* Discipline produces focus. Governance provides structure. A drumbeat provides a regular pace.
- *Baseline every dollar, all the people, all the stuff, and all the capability within the entity and assign accountability for outcomes.* The hardest task is finding the starting point for measuring success. Although some believe this is a mechanical activity, it is a cultural change event.
- *Remove barriers to productivity.* The enterprise team's main activity should be the removal of barriers to forward movement.

Leading the Charge

Creating the Enterprise Effect as described in this chapter requires strong affirmative leadership. To succeed, you need to know where you are today, set a course for the future, and never lower your sights. A leader must also establish a clear, concise message rooted in the Main Thing and a single customer-centric metric and use that metric to guide action at every level—from top to bottom.

Hundreds of books on leadership have been published in recent years. All enumerate the traits and behaviors of competent leaders. We won't bother repeating them here. The Enterprise Effect, however, demands qualities we, and Wally Massenburg, regard as unique. Its leaders must do the following:

- *Leave their egos at the door.* Bringing two or more entities together also brings two or more egos into the room. Leadership must be shared. The hardest thing to overcome is the "who's in charge?" question.

- *Subordinate their personal and organizational concerns to the greater good.* As the leader, you may find this very hard to do. Be guided by the single customer metric.

- *Empathize.* In ordinary circumstances leaders can be single-minded in the pursuit of their goals, but enterprise leadership requires collaboration with others. To collaborate, leaders must understand their counterparts and their concerns.

- *Demonstrate courage.* Bringing different organizations together in service of a common purpose creates doubts and resistance. Courage is required to press forward.

- *Keep people focused on the larger goal.* Everyone involved in the enterprise is a member of another organization (the one that signs his or her paycheck). Attention naturally gravitates toward the goals of their home organizations. The leader must keep them motivated and focused on the goals of the enterprise.

As evidenced in our cases, Big Hat leadership is the catalyst for transformation and alignment. In the Dana-Farber/Children's case, two patient-focused CEOs provided the glue that kept two independent medical institutions and their staffs together and focused on the best possible care for children with cancer. At FedEx, Fred Smith and his executive team have demonstrated year after year how a confederation of businesses can operate superbly under the umbrella of a single brand and with the same high standards. Finally, in our Navy case, two admirals courageously defied years of silo thinking to form a virtual enterprise in service of an important mission.

You will notice that in each case, the move to the Enterprise Effect was triggered by the customer voice and a clear customer need. That need could not be met by a single organization acting alone and with its existing capabilities. And in each case, a leader with a Big Hat heard the customer voice and acted affirmatively.

Key Points on the Enterprise Effect

- Partnering between separate companies can create greater value for both the companies and their common customers.
- Enterprise leadership requires a set of unique behaviors.
- When separate organizations create a virtual organization dedicated to providing greater value to end customers, they achieve the ultimate expression of alignment, the Enterprise Effect.

Things to Do

- Identify a customer or supplier you work with. Use our five partnering questions to create an action plan for working more effectively together.

Epilogue

Now that you've read the details of our method and seen examples of alignment at work, you're probably thinking, "This makes sense on paper, but does it really work in practice, and will alignment help in my situation?" Yes, alignment does produce positive results, and unless your situation is very unusual, experience tells us that it should work for you.

Over the years during which we've been advocating alignment and teaching its methods, we've seen enough before-and-after situations to appreciate its power to improve performance in all types of organizations: manufacturers, service providers, shipping companies, government bodies, and healthcare institutions, to name just a few. We've seen how clients have learned to align and rapidly realign strategy, people, and processes with the needs of their customers, achieving impressive results. Organizations that do it well show measureable business improvement in customer satisfaction, profitability, and employee satisfaction—all at the same time.

Operational improvements like these should be reward enough. However, there's another benefit. The practice of alignment will make you a better, more effective manager: more aware of what's going on, more in control, more able to deal with complexity and change.

As one senior manager told us, "The alignment process and the information it provided gave me incredible insight into the source of our problems—both within the organization and outside with our partners and clients. Detailed drill downs gave us a very focused look at problem areas and made it possible for us to track the impact of actions we took over time."

Said another, "The greatest value of the alignment process was the specific information it gave us. [We were able to] act quicker at the right pulse point to have immediate impact."

An effective alignment process will indicate where your intervention is most needed long before standard measures of operational performance sound the alarm. The capacity to identify points of misalignment and respond to them quickly will enhance your ability to manage in a complex and fast-changing world. More important, the ability to rapidly realign in the face of change will ensure sustainable competitive advantage for your enterprise.

Just as our clients have learned to rapidly realign their organizations, we've learned as well. We've learned that the empirical research supporting the alignment concept, which shows a correlation between alignment and operational performance, is sound. In most cases, we have found a very strong correlation between high alignment scores and high levels of operational performance. The corollary is also true: the poorest performing businesses, military units, and healthcare organizations have the lowest alignment scores.

We've also learned that managers can create alignment by involving people in the process of measurement. Measurement focuses people's attention on the things that matter and thus drives behavior, and behavior creates culture. A culture of alignment continuously improves and sustains the effectiveness and efficiency of customer-centric organizations.

Finally, we've come to appreciate more than ever that alignment is all about leadership. Rapidly aligning an organization requires the positive, affirmative energy of an effective leader. At the heart of every example in this book is a leader who saw the need to refocus and realign and provided the affirmative energy that made it happen. And yes, those leaders put on a Big Hat and had the courage to step up to the challenge. It's not magic. Like the leaders we've described, you can do it too.

Organizational alignment is a solid doctrine. We hope this book has provided you with the tools and insights to implement it and, most especially, the will to step up and lead!

Implementing the Alignment Assessment Tool: A Case Example

One of our early nonbusiness applications of a web-based measurement system was for the U.S. Navy. Admiral Vern Clark, whom you've met in earlier chapters, understood the principles of alignment from our first book but was frustrated by his inability to measure the misalignment he knew was lurking in the vast enterprise he commanded. "Of the five major goals I have for the Navy," he told us, "alignment is the only one I can't measure." Having beta tested a web-based alignment measurement system at FedEx, we explained how we could provide the measurements the Navy needed, and the admiral told us in effect, "Full steam ahead."

The Navy's version of the alignment measurement system was initially tested at the Naval Surface Forces Command in Coronado, California, and Norfolk, Virginia, with the support of its commander, Vice Admiral Tim LaFleur. LaFleur was responsible for providing combat-ready ships for the service. His was a huge command with thousands of military and civilian personnel and operations throughout the world. At his suggestion, our four-dimensional alignment framework was slightly altered. "Those we serve" replaced "customer," and "mission" replaced "strategy." In the end, the Navy assessed alignment across the four primary dimensions of mission, people, processes, and those we serve instead of strategy, people, processes, and customers.

About 600 people representing 18 staff departments in both Coronado and Norfolk were sent an e-mail requesting that they link to a website, where they viewed a 90-second video in which Vice Admiral LaFleur spoke directly to them. He explained Admiral Clark's belief that alignment would help them accomplish the Navy's primary mission—its Main Thing—victory in combat. He went on to stress how their work contributed to the mission of providing combat-ready ships. He asked for their help and requested that they respond to a survey composed of 90 normative statements that were nested in the four dimensions of alignment. That survey also included three open-ended questions with respect to better execution of the command's mission:

What should we start doing?
What should we stop doing?
What should we continue doing?

The respondents were asked to provide some demographic information: pay grade, location, department, gender, and length of service. To ensure confidentiality, a minimum of three individuals had to have the same demographics; otherwise their responses could not be accepted.

Once people had taken the survey and the data were collected, the software instantaneously analyzed and presented the data in three complementary formats:

- *The alignment wheel*, an overview of all elements of alignment and the factors that constitute them
- *The bull's-eye*, which enabled comparisons between demographic elements down to the statement level
- *Gap analysis*, which provided a clear ranking of alignment in either ascending or descending order of demographic units per factor

All formats were color coded in red, yellow, and green (below 55 percent, 55 to 80 percent, and 80 percent and above). Those colors denoted the level of alignment and effective practice, with green being the best. (Since this book is printed in black and white, colors are rendered here in gray scale.)

The Alignment Wheel

The system's alignment wheel screen (Figure A.1) made it possible for Vice Admiral LaFleur to quickly scroll through his 19 departments (using the scroll-down menu in the upper-left corner of the figure) and easily identify best-demonstrated practices for each factor. The department shown here, N1, was the command's manpower office at Norfolk, which had good to excellent scores.

The alignment wheel also made it possible for LaFleur to quickly identify pockets of misalignment and subpar performance. Figure A.2 shows the scores of a department whose overall score was significantly lower than any of the others. With 40 people, the department was typical in size. However, the profusion of low scores (shown as light gray) among a number of factors indicated general dissatisfaction and misalignment. There was enough information in that wheel to tell the leadership that action was needed.

NOTE

The assessment tool described in this appendix was initially developed by the authors' firm, ODI, using then-off-the-shelf software and the help of outside programmers. It has since been enhanced and improved by InfoTool (www.infotool-online.com) and is InfoTool's proprietary product.

Since the normative statements that make up the assessment define the way the enterprise *should function*, they provide leadership with a clear, prescriptive set of organizational and managerial behaviors.

FIGURE A. 1 ALIGNMENT ASSESSMENT WHEEL

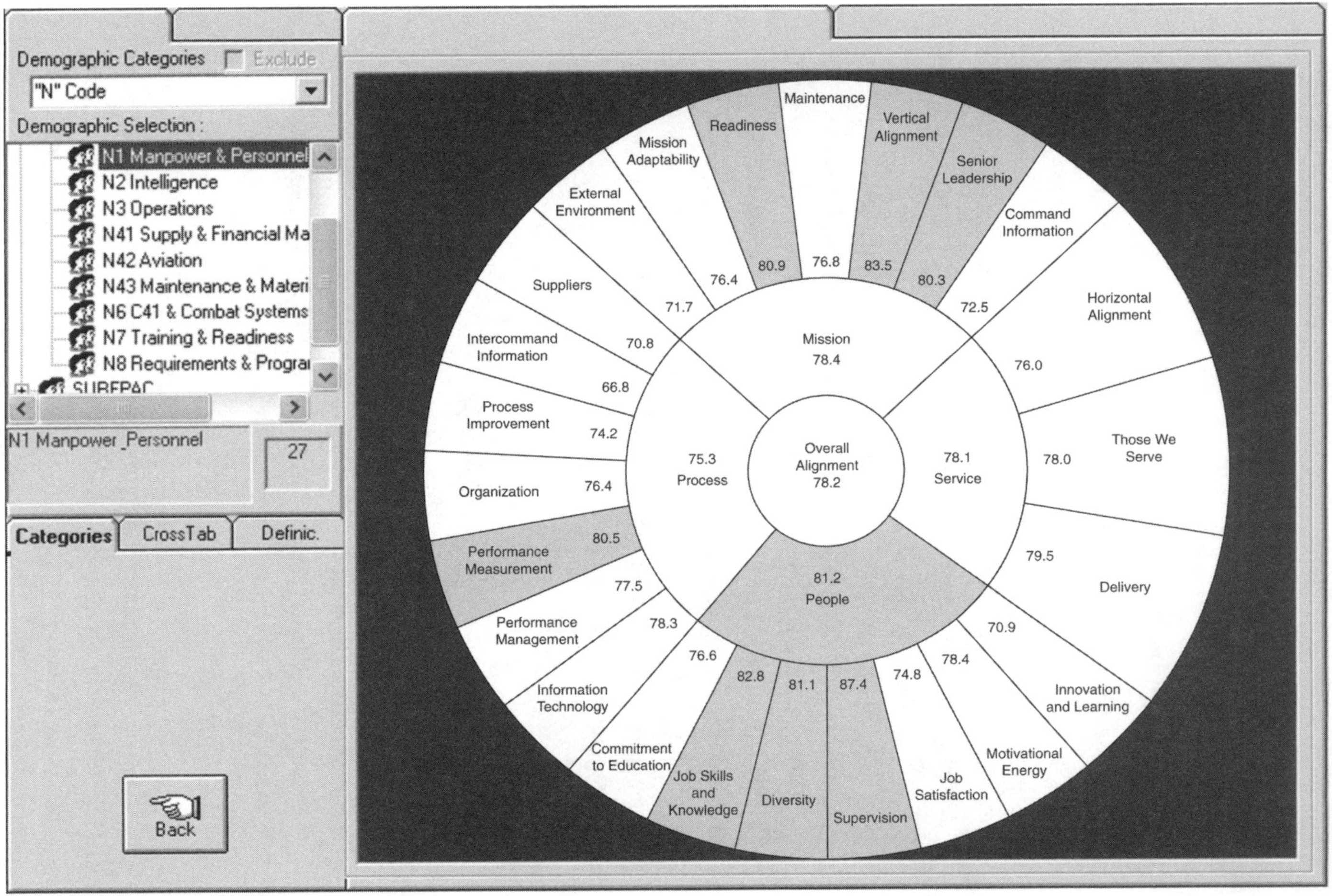

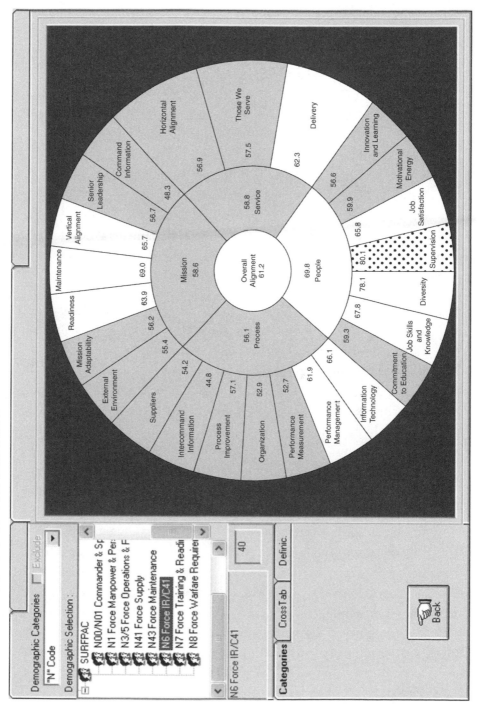

We mentioned earlier that the system allows users to drill down below the level of aggregated data. A cross-tab feature in the software allows one to combine any of the demographic elements such as pay grade and department or length of service and gender. In this particular application, it was helpful to gain a better understanding of the problems and their sources by drilling down into the data and examining the responses of different pay grades within the department. Drilling down revealed that the problems were not spread equally among the 40 people in the department. Figure A.3 clearly indicates that 12 individuals with the ranks of E7 to E9, the highest enlisted ranks, were skewing the overall score of the department. Armed with this knowledge, the leaders were able to take highly targeted corrective actions.

The Bull's-Eye

The bull's-eye representation of the data permits comparisons of various demographic elements, such as departments. It also can drill down to take those comparisons to the statement level. For example, Figure A.4 shows a comparison between two of LaFleur's personnel departments: Norfolk (the innermost line) and its counterpart in Coronado (the outermost line). These two departments were doing the same things, and each had 27 people. This screen examines one of the 24 factors of alignment on the wheel: process improvement. Its normative statements related to waste, reviewing methods, creating process champions, and so on. Norfolk was clearly performing better in each of the elements related to process improvement. After seeing this chart, the captain in charge of the Coronado department phoned her counterpart in Norfolk. Together they scrolled through each factor and focused on areas where there was significant misalignment. The Coronado captain asked, "What are you doing in Norfolk that I'm not doing here?" Using that information and her own analysis of the data, she took immediate and effective corrective action. Nine months later, after the second assessment, her alignment scores were higher than those of her colleagues in Norfolk.

FIGURE A.3   DRILLING DOWN

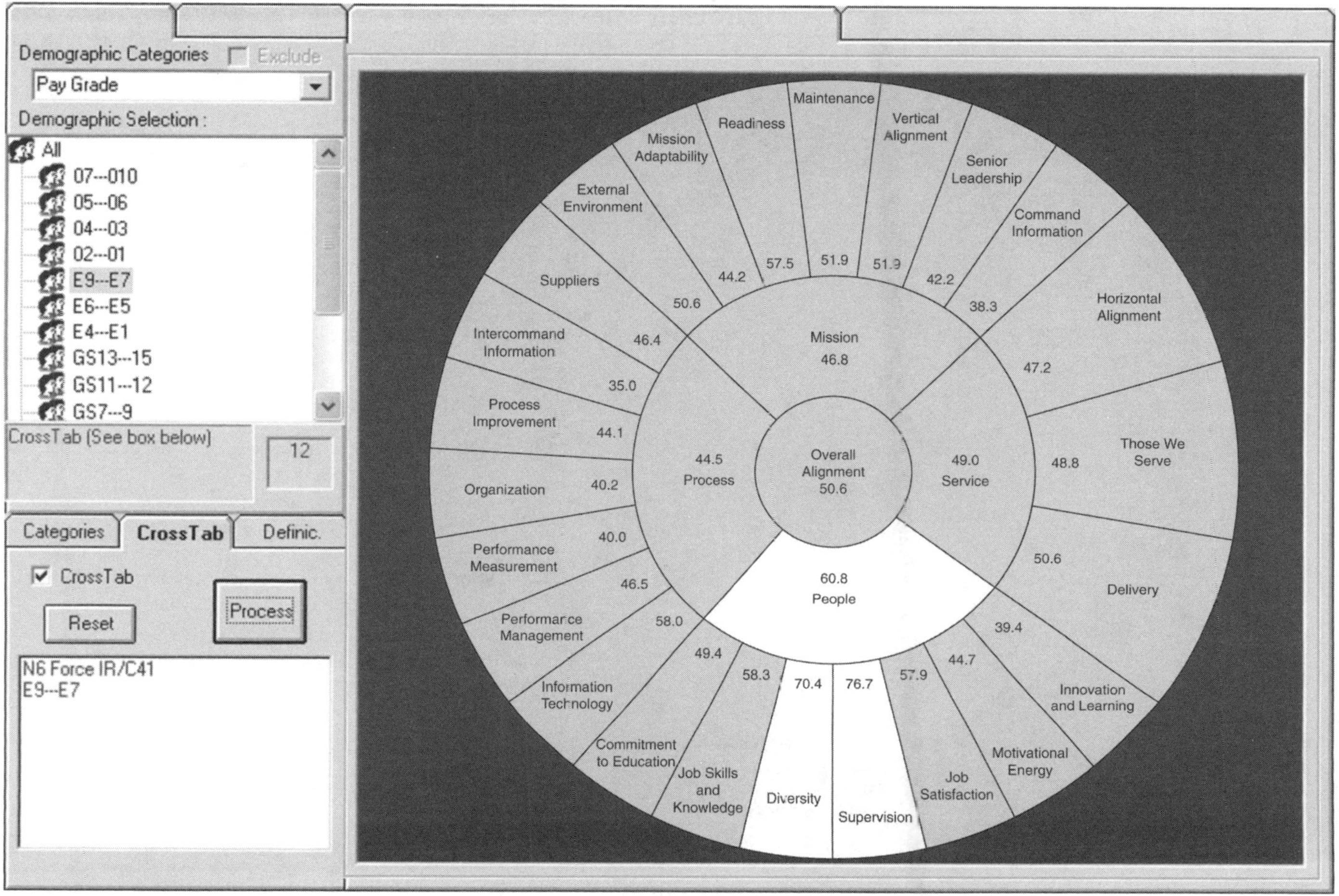

FIGURE A.4 TWO PERSONNEL DEPARTMENTS COMPARED

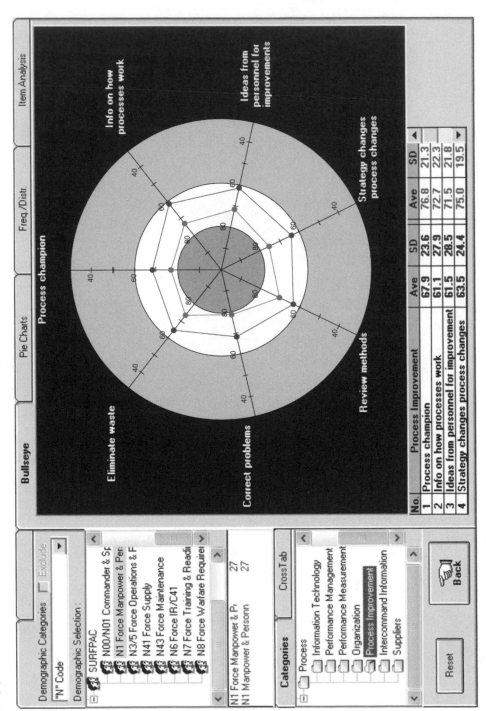

Gap Analysis

Gap analysis is another way of quickly identifying best practices that can be shared and problem areas that demand managerial attention. For the leaders we've worked with, the gap analysis screen is a popular data display; it provides a quick comparison and ranking for any demographic element. In the case of Admiral LaFleur's group, for example, it ranked each department against its peers elsewhere in the command. For department leaders (and ship captains) it answered the question that every Type A department leader and every skipper wanted to know: Where do I stand relative to my peers? The gap analysis screen shot in Figure A.5 ranks the departments in LaFleur's command against the factor of performance measurement. By scrolling through the 24 factors, LaFleur could see which departments were clustered at the top and which were consistently at the bottom.

The admiral provided each of his commanders with the results of gap analysis as well as the analysis engine that enabled them to do their own comparisons. When we asked him what he was going to do about particularly troubled departments, he said, "Nothing. I don't have to do anything, because *they* [the department heads] know that *I* know." And so did their peers.

Toward Realignment

The insights gained through the assessment and subsequent analysis led to many changes in the sprawling command. Over a nine-month period, every department and unit leader took action. Armed with solid data, each knew where his or her operations were strong and weak—and knew that his or her peers also knew.

At the end of the nine-month period, personnel went back to their computers, logged into the assessment tool site, and took the survey anew. Once again, the results were recorded and displayed in graphic form for all to see. What they saw assured them that all those meetings, best practice sharing, and improvement efforts had been worth the effort. Figure A.6 shows before and after views of the alignment wheel for the troubled department shown in Figure A.2. For most of

FIGURE A.5 GAP ANALYSIS OF PERFORMANCE MANAGEMENT BY DEPARTMENT

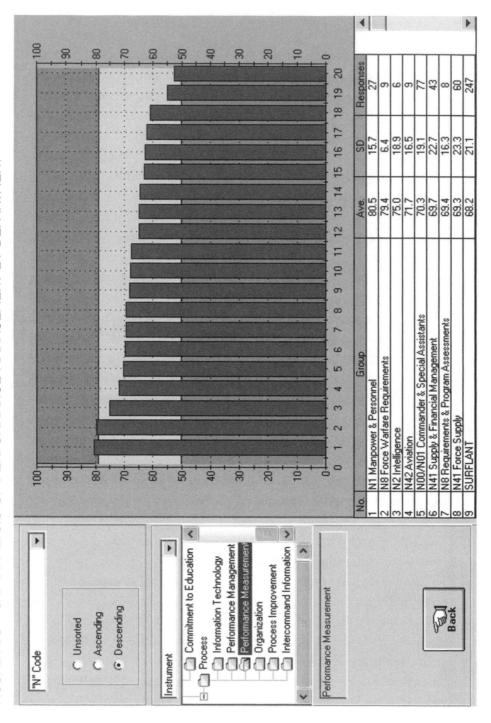

FIGURE A.6A   THE ALIGNMENT WHEEL, BEFORE

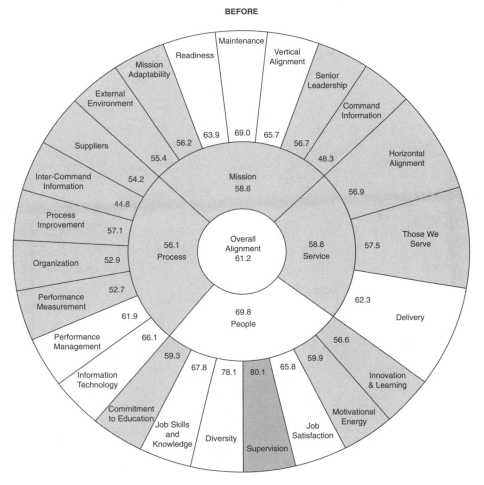

the departments, the improvements were noted in almost every factor and in every dimension of alignment. These results were achieved by providing leaders with relevant and timely information.

More importantly, naval battle groups, the command's "customers," rated the command's services to them as being significantly improved.

FIGURE A.6B   THE ALIGNMENT WHEEL, AFTER

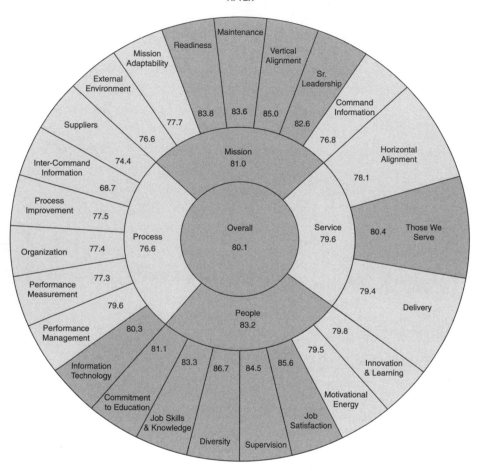

Notes

Chapter 2

1. Steven Kerr, "On the Folly of Hoping for A While Rewarding B," *Academy of Management Journal*, December 1975, p. 18.

Chapter 3

1. William H. Massy and Benjamin Schneider, "The Meaning of Employee Engagement," *Industrial and Organizational Psychology*, No. 1, 2008, pp. 3–30.
2. Gallup, Inc., "Employee Engagement," poll report, 2010, p. 3.
3. See Michael Lee Stallard and Jason Pankau, "To Boost Performance, Connect with the Core," *Leader to Leader*, Summer 2010, p. 51.
4. Hay Group, "Engage Employees and Boost Performance," Working Paper, 2001.

Chapter 4

1. Eric von Hippel, *Sources of Innovation*. New York and Oxford: Oxford University Press, 1987.
2. Amanda Craig, Charlese Jones, and Martha Nieto, "Fashion Follower—Industry Leader," Philadelphia University, April 2004.

3. A number of case studies have been written about Zara, its business model, and its IT system over the last dozen years. Perhaps the most complete is Pankaj Ghemawat and José Luis Nueno, "Zara: Fast Fashion," Boston: Harvard Business Publishing, Case 9–703–497, revised December 21, 2006.

4. Ghemawat and Nueno, "Zara: Fast Fashion," Ibid.

5. U.S. General Accounting Office, "Management Practices: U.S. Companies Improve Performance Through Quality Efforts," May 1991.

6. George Labovitz and Victor Rosansky, *The Power of Alignment*. New York: Wiley, 1997, p. 117.

Chapter 5

1. W. Edwards Deming, *Out of Crisis*. Cambridge, MA: MIT Center for Advanced Educational Services, 1986. This landmark book and its 14 points was intended to transform the management of U.S. manufacturing, which was being decimated by Japanese competitors. The book is often credited as the launching pad for the Total Quality Management movement.

2. Charles Duhigg and Keith Bradsher, "How the U.S. Lost Out on iPhone Work," *New York Times*, January 21, 2012.

Chapter 6

1. For more information on Walmart's use of social media, see http://www.internalcommshub.com/open/channels/casestudies/walmart.shtml <accessed 4 April 2012>.

2. See http://www.internalcommshub.com/open/channels/casestudies/walmart.shtml <accessed 4 April 2012>.

3. Or go to http://mystarbucksidea.force.com/ideaList?ext=0&lsi=0&category=Food <accessed 2 April 2012>.

4. A print or free downloadable version of the book *Democratizing Innovation* can be ordered through http://web.mit.edu/evhippel/www/books.htm. Or you can search YouTube for von Hippel's lectures on this topic.

Chapter 7

1. See Zappos.com website, "Zappo's Family Core Value #2."
2. Lou Gerstner, *Who Says Elephants Can't Dance? Inside IBM's Historic Turnaround*. New York: HarperCollins, 2003.
3. James Heskett, *The Culture Cycle: How to Shape the Unseen Force That Transforms Performance*. New York: FT Press, 2011.
4. Barry Jaruzelski, John Loehr, and Richard Holman, "Why Culture Is Key," *Strategy + Business*, No. 65, Winter 2011.
5. For more on Pixar, see Ed Catmull, "How Pixar Fosters Collective Creativity." *Harvard Business Review*, September 2008.

Chapter 8

1. Paul Leinwand and Cesare Mainardi, *The Essential Advantage: How to Win with a Capabilities-Driven Strategy* (Boston: Harvard Business Review Press, 2011).
2. Our colleague at the Boston University School of Management, Professor John McCarthy has written cases about Ingar Skaug and Wilhelmsen Lines. We often use them in class to demonstrate the application of the Slow-Fast-Faster process organizational transformation. This synopsis is used with his permission.

Chapter 9

1. This information is based on FedEx's operating manual (February 20, 2011), which the company kindly shared with us.
2. Frederick W. Smith and William G. Margaritas, "The Reputational Intelligence Reward," www.chiefexecutive.net, May–June 2010.

Index

About the Authors

Dr. George H. Labovitz is the founder and CEO of ODI, an international management training and consulting company, and professor of management and organizational behavior at the Boston University School of Management (glabovitz@orgdynamics.com).

Victor Rosansky, former executive vice president of ODI, is cofounder and president of LHR International, Inc. He has more than 25 years experience as a consultant, helping Fortune 500 clients to drive rapid strategy deployment and alignment (victor@LHR international.com).